Handmade Bags
in
Natural Fabrics

60 Easy-to-Make
Purses, Totes
and More

Emiko Takahashi

TUTTLE Publishing

Tokyo │ Rutland, Vermont │ Singapore

PLEASE NOTE:

The bags in this book are designed to be sewn by hand, though most of the steps can be completed by machine. For those steps that require hand sewing or for any project that you would like to hand sew from beginning to end, thread that is specifically intended for hand sewing is recommended. These threads tend to be stronger and are less likely to knot as you work. Hand sewing threads should not be used in your sewing machine.

All-purpose threads intended for both hand and machine sewing can also be used. As with any sewing project, care should be taken to choose the right thread for your fabric. If using these threads to hand sew (especially when sewing seams and gussets or attaching handles), a little beeswax worked into the thread will add smoothness and strength.

Measurements in this book are given in both inches and metrics unless otherwise noted. The metric measurements are more precise, and using them if possible will result in a better finish.

AUTHOR'S FOREWORD

Hand-stitched bags are soft and easy to use. Create the handles and straps the width and length to suit you and the bags will mold themselves to your body, resulting in a treasured item you can use for years.

The sewing process has been designed to be simple even for beginners.

It's fun sewing the front and back of a bag together, then turning it right side out. Take it easy and enjoy your sewing time, guiding a needle in and out through fabric that's pleasant to touch.

Why not pick up a sewing needle and make a start?

Emiko Takahashi

Contents

part 1
Shopping Bags

01.
Contrasting Fabric Bag with Handles

The simple design of this bag in neutral brown shades makes it easy to match
to any outfit. It's made from knit fabric matched with check tweed.
Instructions on page 43

02.
Lace Appliqué Bag with Handles

Mini motifs have been appliquéd onto this bag that's made in a warm tweed fabric. The pocket edging and bag opening have been decorated with lace to bring out the sweet appeal of the round shape.
Instructions on page 44

Position motifs as you like to achieve a balanced look, then stitch them on.

03.
Two-way Bag

What sets this bag apart is the two sets of handles of different lengths attached to the bag's inside. Even if you use one set of handles, the other remains conveniently hidden inside. Cut the shoulder straps and handles to the right length for your height.
Instructions on page 45

1 Place in shopping basket

2 Place checked out items in bag

3 Pull drawstrings closed and go!

0 4.

Checkout Basket Bag

Set this bag into a supermarket basket when you get to the cash register and your shopping can be checked out and placed straight into the bag. All you have to do is pull the drawstrings shut and you're ready to go. Great as a laundry bag too—there are plenty of ways to use this design.

Instructions on pages 46–47

05

06

07

08

09

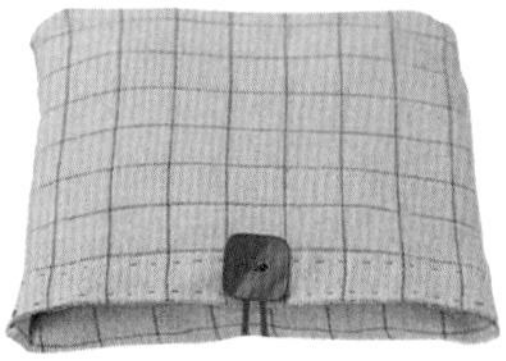

Fold down to size, insert body of bag into pocket and do up the button—the bag becomes a compact pouch.

05. ～ 10.
Eco Bag

Plenty can fit in these large bags. The handles are wide so it's easy to carry heavy things. Make a few in different fabrics or with different buttons to match your outfits.
Instructions on pages 48–49

10

11, 12.

Reversible Bags—Full-circle Bag and Puff-out Tuck Bag

11 is made from a circular piece of material which becomes a bag when the straps are drawn up.
12 has tucks in the base to create a gently rounded shape. Generous proportions make for ease
of use. Reversibility is an added plus. Choose which side to display depending on your mood.

Instructions for bag 11 on pages 50–51; for bag 12 on pages 52–53

11

12

part 2
Everyday Bags

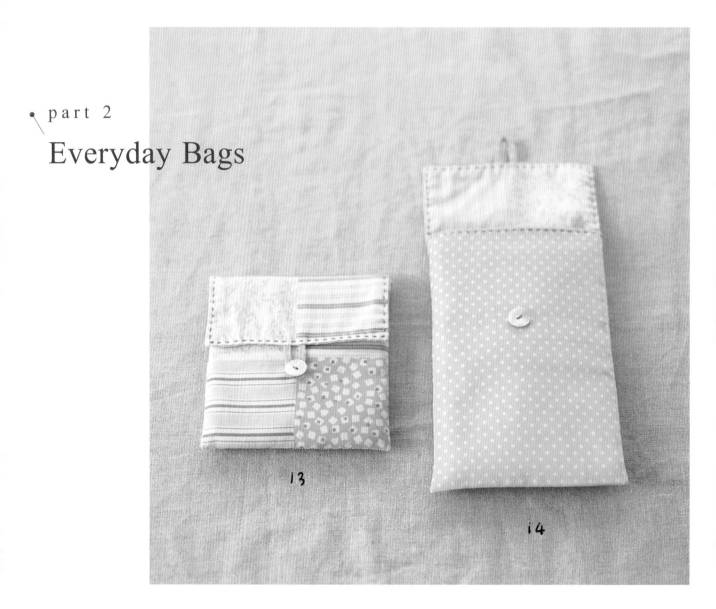

13

i4

15

16

13. ~ 16.
Little Purse and Shoulder Bag with Flaps, Both in Small and Large Sizes

This design makes use of the number of squares in the patchwork pattern, with the edge of the patch-work pieces creating guidelines for easy cutting and stitching. It's created by folding outer and inner bag pieces like origami, then matching them together. The button loops peeking out add a cute touch.

Instructions for bags 13 & 14 on page 58, for bags 15 & 16 on pages 56–57

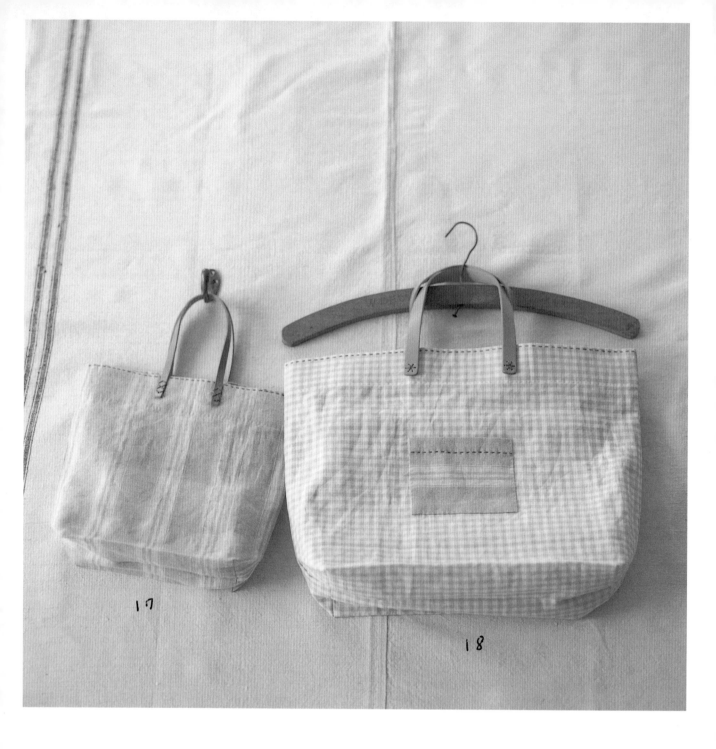

17. 18.
Tote Bag with Gusset (S, L)

The linen used in this design gets softer with each wash.
These bags are just the right size for running errands.
Leather has been used for the handles.
Instructions on pages 35 and 70

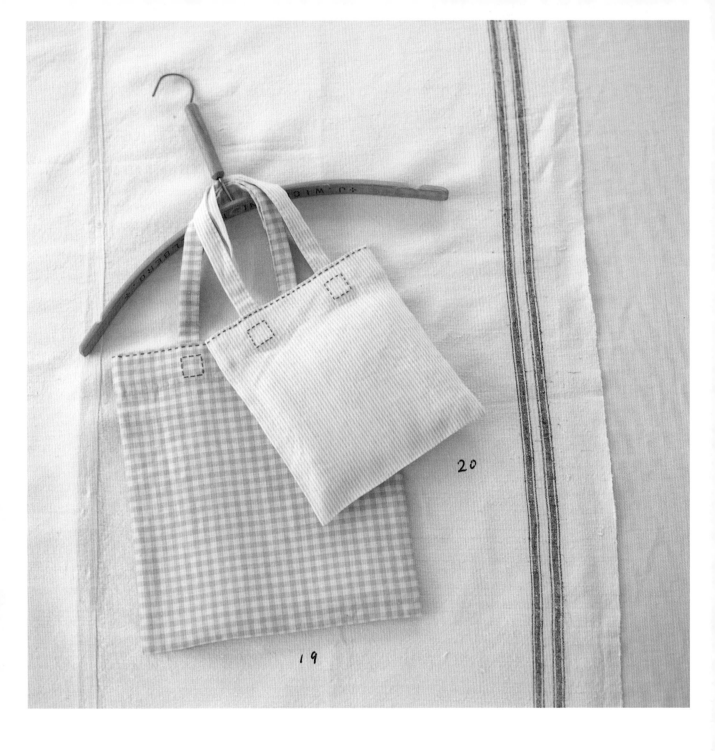

19. 20.

Flat Bag (S, L)

With their basic "bag" shape, these easy-to-use bags are recommended for beginners. Made from only one piece of fabric, the fold becomes the base, and stitches in stand-out shades emphasize the simple design.

Instructions on pages 34–35

21.

Long Tote with Floral Motifs

The fashionable long rectangular shape and ease of use makes this a popular design. Made from floral print corduroy, the flower motif on the handles and the eye-catching stitching at the motif's center are cute accents.

Instructions on page 59

Wind wool around thick card to create pompom.

22.

Tote with Pompom

A pompom made of felt and wool creates a warm look for this bag, which is a simple design using one piece of felt fabric. As it's made from felt, it's not necessary to finish off the edges. The handles are crocheted from the same wool as the pompom.

Instructions on page 60

23

24

Apply appliqué fabric
to the bag and stitch.

25

23. ~ 25.
Picnic Tote (S, M, L)

As the inner and outer fabrics for this bag are both linen,
it has some body to it already, but the shape is retained by
using belt interfacing around the opening and a board in
the base. This versatile bag lends itself to all kinds of uses.
Instructions on pages 61–62

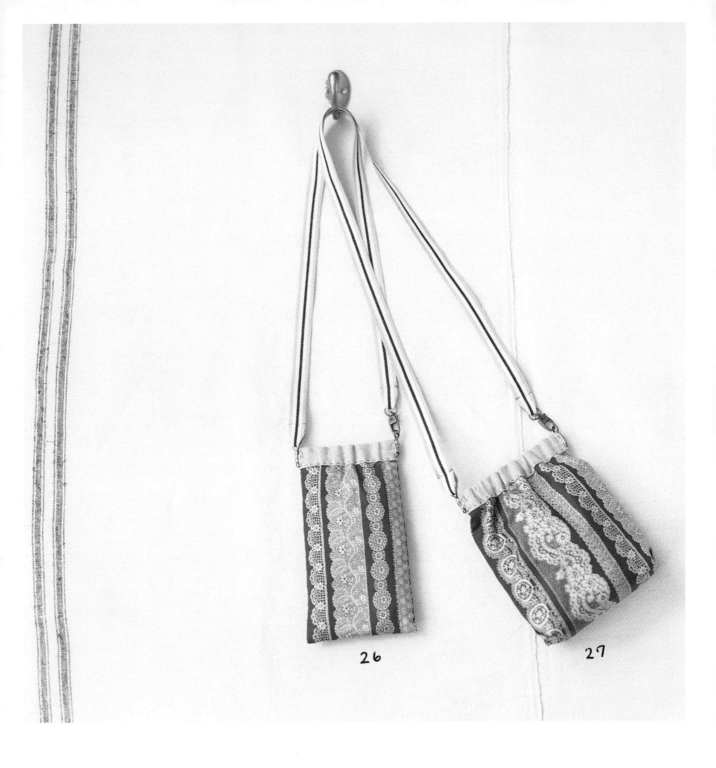

26

27

26. ~ 29.

Purse and Shoulder Bag with Spring Clasp

The relaxed, grown-up color combination of this lace print makes it easy to use with
any outfit. Cut the shoulder strap longer if you want to wear the bag at waist length.

Instructions on pages 63–64

28

29

30. ～ 38.
Little Fancy Purse in Soft Fabric

This purse has a sweet, rounded shape when the strings are drawn. Made from two pieces of fabric, it's easily decorated with beads, your favorite buttons or ribbons.

Instructions on pages 36–37 and pages 54–55

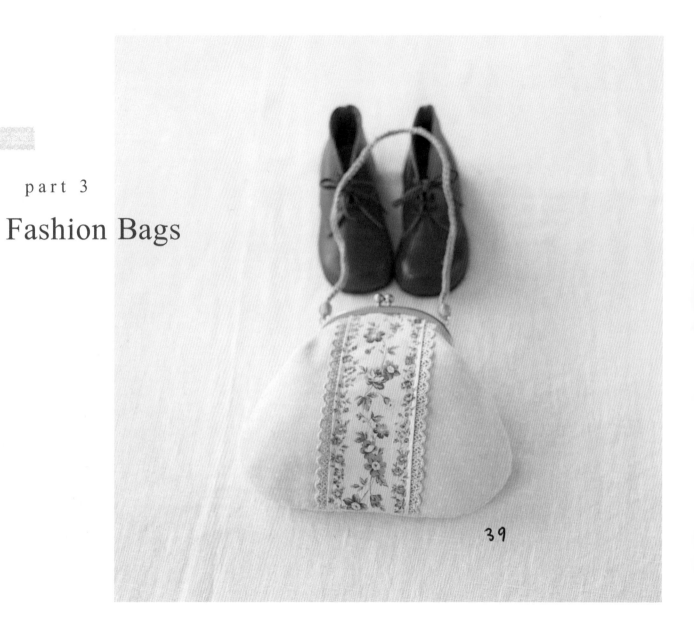

part 3

Fashion Bags

40

39.40.
Bag with Frame

There's a whiff of nostalgia to this bag with its frame and cute, voluminous shape. Appliqué made from floral material has been added to accent the soft double-layer gauze. The handles crocheted from hand sewing thread add a gentle touch.

Instructions for bag 39 on pages 65–66, for bag 40 on page 67

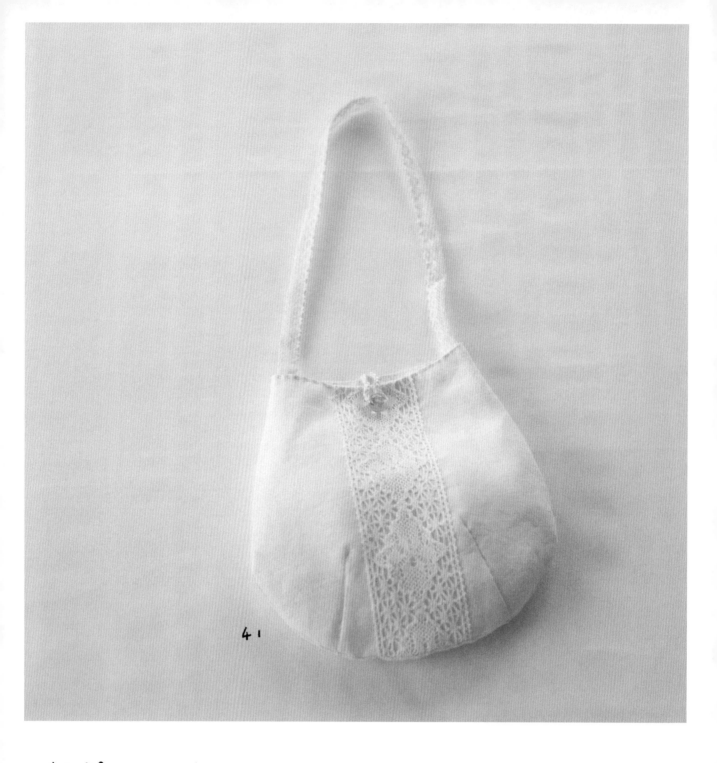

41

41. 42.
Small Bag

The soft, pretty, see-through patterns of this cotton voile are perfect for hand stitching. A glass bead has been used as a closure on one version, while the other has glass beads and a tassel. A lace strap or one made from glass beads strung onto crocheted hand sewing thread add gentle expression.
Instructions on pages 68–69

42

43

The charm of self-cover
buttons is that you can use
whatever fabric you like!

43. 44.
Bag with Lace-trim Zipper (S, L)

The shape of this bag allows it to fit perfectly to your body when worn on the shoulder. The well-formed gussets mean even the small version has room for everything you need to carry. Both inner and outer layers are linen, with fusible bag interfacing creating a sturdy finished product. Add buttons covered in check fabric or sequins and lines of stitching for a fashionable touch.

Instructions on pages 71–73

44

45. ~ 58.

Vase-shaped Bag

The curved lines of this bag are real attention-grabbers. The trick to creating an attractive silhouette is to cut the fusible quilt wadding to the bag's finished size. The decorations are up to you: sequins, beads, embroidery, appliqué—let your imagination run wild.

Instructions on pages 74–75

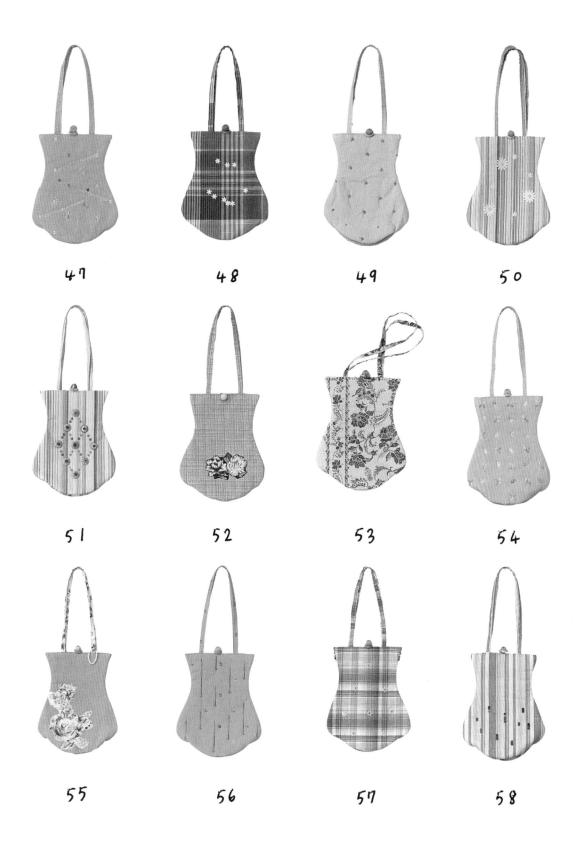

47

48

49

50

51

52

53

54

55

56

57

58

Cut a flower shape from
scrap fabric, sew around
it and gather stitches.

59.
Tucked Bag with Corsage

Made from the same fabric as the bag, the corsage decoration is created
by simply sewing all around a flower shape and drawing up the threads.
Fusible interfacing allows it to retain a nice shape.

Instructions on pages 76–77

60.

Tucked Bag with Floral Embroidery

The pale pink tones used in this bag seem to inspire kind, calm feelings.
Floral embroidery is added as an accent. A magnet has been attached
inside as a closure.

Instructions on pages 78–79

19. 20. Flat Bag

Photo: page 15

● MATERIALS FOR 19

Gingham (for the outer fabric and handles)
20 x 28 in (50 x 70cm)
Fusible belt interfacing 1⅛ in wide x 22 in
    (3cm wide x 55cm)
Hand sewing thread such as MOCO brand, brown
Hand sewing thread such as Schappe Spun
    brand, beige

● MATERIALS FOR 20

Striped fabric (for the outer fabric and handles)
    16 x 24 in (40 x 60cm)
Fusible belt interfacing 1⅛ in wide x 16 in
    (3cm wide x 40cm)
Hand sewing thread such as MOCO brand, brown
Hand sewing thread such as Schappe Spun
    brand, beige

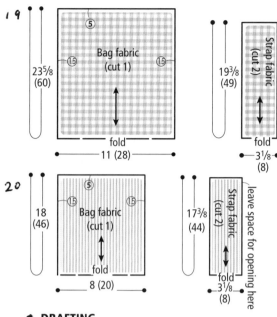

● DRAFTING

※ Measurements given in inches and centimeters
※○ Add figure in circle as seam allowance when
    drafting pattern
    (①cm = ⅜ in; ⑮cm = ⅝ in; ⑤cm = 2 in)

● INSTRUCTIONS (the bag shown here is no. 20)

CREATE BAG

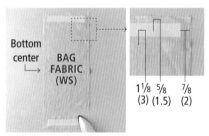

1 Cut out the fabric for the bag. Using a dry iron on a medium setting, bond the fusible belt interfacing to the opening edges of the bag.

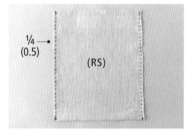

2 Fold fabric in half with wrong sides facing and sew sides using running stitch (see p41, 42 for sewing instructions).

CREATE STRAPS AND ATTACH TO BAG

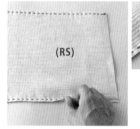

3 Using your fingernails, press the seam open. Following the stitching line, press the seam allowance back to create a fold line (see p42 for sewing instructions).

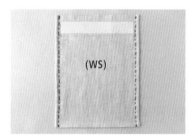

4 Turn bag so wrong side faces out and backstitch along finished stitching line to create a French seam (see p42 for sewing instructions).

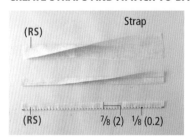

5 Fold strips of fabric in half so that wrong sides meet and a fold line is created. Fold fabric edges to meet along center and fold in half again. Stitch through all thicknesses along edge.

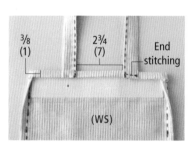

6 Matching symbols, pin straps into position on bag opening. Sew to seam allowance of bag opening using running stitch.

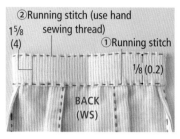

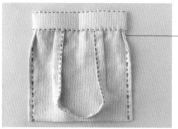

②Running stitch (use hand sewing thread)

1⅝ (4)

①Running stitch

⅛ (0.2)

BACK (WS)

Fold seam allowance to back

7 Fold 1⅝ in (4cm) of bag opening over to wrong side and stitch in order ①running stitch (use hand sewing thread) ②running stitch (use hand sewing thread). (See p55 for embroidery instructions). Fold both side seam allowances to the back.

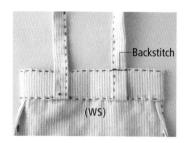

Backstitch

(WS)

8 Fold straps back up and pin in place. Sew using backstitch (see p42 for sewing instructions).

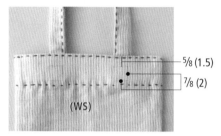

⅝ (1.5)

⅞ (2)

(WS)

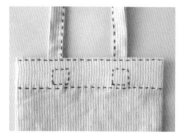

9 Turn bag right-side out. Mark position of decorative stitching for straps using fabric pencil.

10 Sew decorative stitching through one layer of outer fabric using hand sewing thread.

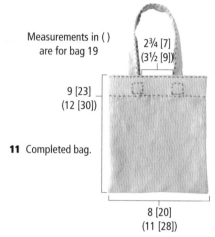

Measurements in ( ) are for bag 19

2¾ [7]
(3½ [9])

9 [23]
(12 [30])

8 [20]
(11 [28])

11 Completed bag.

It's in the Details

17. 18. Master Sewing a Gusset

● **INSTRUCTIONS** (the bag shown here is no. 18)

Photo: page 14 instructions: page 70

CREATE BAG, SEW GUSSETS

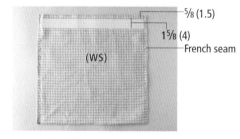

⅝ (1.5)

1⅝ (4)

French seam

(WS)

1 Create bag (sew as per steps 1–4 for "how to make bag no. 20" on p34)

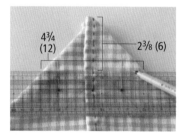

4¾ (12)

2⅜ (6)

2 Bring side seams to meet base, creating a triangle. Mark gusset width with fabric pencil.

3 Using running stitch, sew gusset. Repeat for other side. (see p42 for sewing instructions).

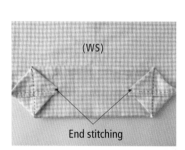

(WS)

End stitching

4 Fold gussets in towards center of base and stitch in place. Attach handles.

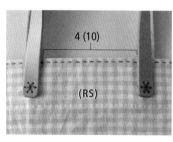

4 (10)

(RS)

5 Working from the center hole out, stitch the leather handles to the bag with hand-sewing thread.

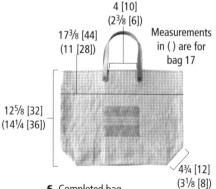

4 [10]
(2⅜ [6])

17⅜ [44]
(11 [28])

Measurements in ( ) are for bag 17

12⅝ [32]
(14¼ [36])

4¾ [12]
(3⅛ [8])

6 Completed bag.

30. ∼ 38. Little Fancy Purse in Soft Fabric

Photo: page 22–23

● MATERIALS

Voile (for outer fabric) 18 x 8 in (45 x 20cm)
Linen (for inner fabric) 18 x 10 (45 x 25cm)
Organza ribbon ⅝ in wide x 36 in (1.5cm wide x 90cm)
Glass bead 10mm (1cm) diameter x two
Hand sewing thread (fine), pink

USE FULL-SIZE PATTERN PIECE SIDE A

※ Measurements given in inches and centimeters
※○ Add figure in circle as seam allowance when drafting pattern
(①cm = ⅜ in; ②cm= ⅞ in)

● INSTRUCTIONS (the bag shown here is no. 31)

SEW BAG PIECES TOGETHER

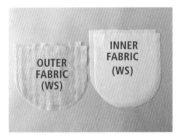

1 Cut two pieces each for both outer and lining fabrics. Match outer fabric pieces with right sides facing and inner fabric pieces in the same way.

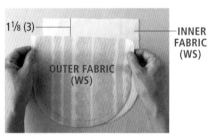

2 Match the pieces from step 1.

3 With all four fabric pieces layered together, pin through all thicknesses with pinheads facing to center of bag.

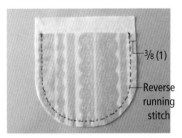

4 Stitch around the edge, using reverse running stitch (see p42 for sewing instructions).

CREATE CASING

5 Make a diagonal cut into the seam allowance of one layer of the lining fabric.

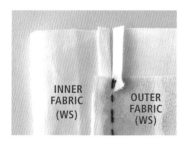

6 Open out seam of lining fabric.

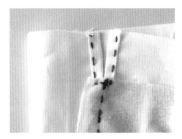

7 Fold seam fabric under twice and secure with running stitch (see p42 for sewing instructions).

8 Clip curves, snipping out V-shaped sections to ensure seam doesn't become too bulky when turned to inside of bag.

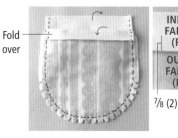

Fold over

INNER FABRIC (RS)
OUTER FABRIC (RS)

⅞ (2)

9 Fold bag opening over twice.

INNER FABRIC (RS)
OUTER FABRIC (RS)

10 Turn bag right side out.

② Backstitch
① Side seam
⅛ (0.2)

11 Stitch along the casing in the order shown, sewing 2–3 times over casing opening.

THREAD CORD THROUGH CASING

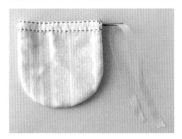

12 Using the ribbon threader, thread one piece of ribbon through each casing.

Glass Bead

13 Attach a glass bead to the ends of ribbon on each side and knot together.

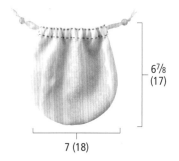

6⅞ (17)

7 (18)

14 Completed bag.

How to Do Embroidery Stitches Used on Purse

GUIDING MARKS FOR EMBROIDERY

① ② ③

For both lazy daisy and double cross stitch, mark fabric using a fabric pencil in the order shown.

LAZY DAISY STITCH
(Used in no. 35)

① ② ③

To make neat lazy daisy stitches, create petals in the order ①. top, bottom ②. left, right ③. diagonals.

DOUBLE CROSS STITCH
(Used in no. 36)

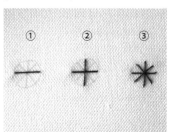

① ② ③

Work in the order ①. left to right ②. top to bottom ③. diagonals to create a neat double cross.

Before You Start

(Have these easy-to-use bits and pieces on hand before you begin)

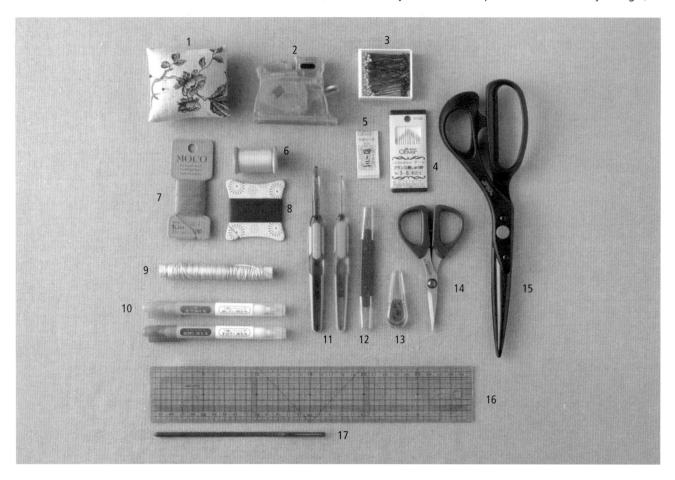

1 Pincushion
Choose one the right size for you.

2 Automatic Threader
This will thread your needle with just the touch of a button.

3 Glass Headed Pins
These extremely fine pins are the best choice for silk fabrics. Their glass heads can withstand the heat of an iron.

4 Embroidery Needles
These fine-tipped needles make for extremely smooth sewing.

5 Sewing Needles
Needles that can sew light- to regular-weight fabrics.

6–9 Hand Sewing Threads
Such as Pice (6) 100% polyester fine sewing thread, best for sewing thin fabrics MOCO (7) 100% polyester heavy sewing thread, excellent for embroidery, stitching and attaching straps Schappe Spun (8) 100% polyester sewing thread. Soie et (9) gradated color silk embroidery thread.

10 Fabric Chalk
Choose a type that rinses out in water or one that fades by itself.

11 Crochet Hook
8mm and size 7/0.

12 Double-headed Threader
This works for both heavy and fine needles.

13 Embroidery Needle Threader
These are designed specifically for embroidery floss/thread.

14 Small Scissors
The sharp tips make these just right for detailed work.

15 Fabric Scissors
These are specifically for cutting fabric.

16 Plotting Scale
The green section allows measurements to be seen even when laid on top of light colored or patterned fabric.

17 Cord Threader
These are made from a smooth material to allow ribbons or cords to pass through casing quickly.

About the Fusible Interfacing and Wadding Used in This Book

Applying fusible interfacing to fabric gives it more body and durability. Make sure you choose the right kind depending on your purpose and needs. Quilt wadding adds airy volume to thin fabrics. For hand sewing, use a lightweight type or fusible wadding.

HOW TO APPLY FUSIBLE INTERFACING

Using a dry iron on medium heat, work from the top down, pressing the iron firmly on each spot for about 10 seconds. Move the iron a little at a time to make sure all parts of the fabric are covered.

1 Heat-bondable double-sided sheet. Convenient for appliqué.

2 Fusible interfacing for straps. Allows you to create straight, neat bag straps.

3 Soft fusible interfacing. Applying fusible interfacing prevents fraying when pattern pieces are cut out and creates an attractive silhouette.

4 Fusible belt interfacing. Applied to the opening of a bag, this interfacing creates a strong, sturdy result even if the item is sewn by hand.

↓

Also used in no. 46

↓

Also used in no. 15

↓

↓

Also used in nos. 1, 3, 17–20, 23–25, 45–58, 60.

5 Smooth fusible interfacing. Applied to a bag, this creates a smooth tautness and allows the bag to keep its shape.

6 Wadding (lightweight). This adds body and volume to soft fabrics such as gauze.

7 Fusible wadding (medium weight). Creates an even, full silhouette.

↓

Also used in no. 44

↓

Also used in no. 40

↓

Also used in nos. 45–58

Polyester interfacing for bags and hats, used in the base of a bag, allows the bag to retain its shape and makes it sturdier.

Used in nos. 21–25, 43, 44, 59, 60

● Handles and Straps Used in This Book

One of the enjoyable things about sewing bags by hand is that various effects can be achieved depending on your choice of straps or handles.
In this book, apart from fabric, leather, wide ribbon and sturdy loop cord have been used. Make a totally original creation by matching whichever strap you like to the shape, fabric and pattern of the bag.

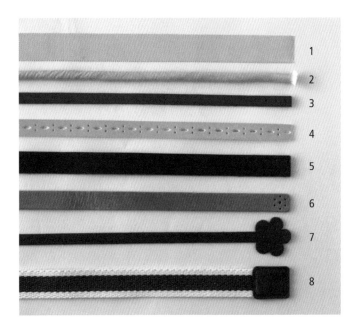

1   Ribbon, items 3 & 4
2   Cord, item 11
3   Leather strip (narrow), item 43
4   Punched leather tape, items 23, 25, 59 & 60
5   6-hole punched leather strip, item 44
6   7-hole punched leather strip, item 18
7   Leather strip with flower motif, item 21
8   Woven tape, item 1

● Clasps and Attachments Used in This Book

These items are easy to incorporate into hand sewing

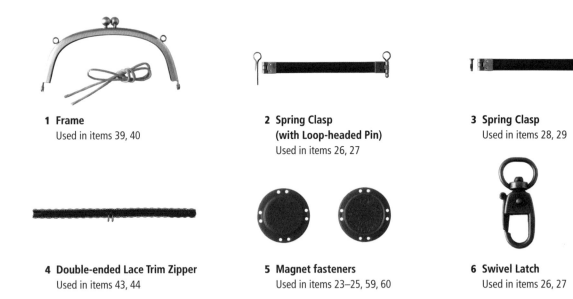

1 Frame
Used in items 39, 40

2 Spring Clasp
(with Loop-headed Pin)
Used in items 26, 27

3 Spring Clasp
Used in items 28, 29

4 Double-ended Lace Trim Zipper
Used in items 43, 44

5 Magnet fasteners
Used in items 23–25, 59, 60

6 Swivel Latch
Used in items 26, 27

● Sewing Basics

The terms and methods for smooth hand sewing are explained here in easy-to-follow diagrams. Once you've learned them, you can get started on making a bag.

MATCH RIGHT SIDES

Layer fabric so patterned sides (right sides of fabric) face one another.

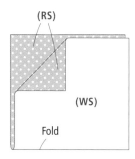

GRAIN

The direction that the warp (vertical threads) run in woven fabric is called the grain. It's hard to pull fabric out of shape along the grain, so outer layers of fabric and handles are cut with this in mind.

SELVAGE

The edges of woven fabric are called the selvage.

DOUBLE FOLD

When fabric is folded over twice to form three layers of fabric it is called a double fold. This is used for casings or to finish off edges.

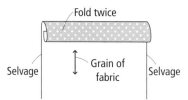

THREAD LENGTH

The ideal length of thread for hand sewing is about 6 in (15cm) longer than your bent elbow when holding the needle up in your hand. It's usual to sew with a single thread only (ie don't knot ends of thread together).

MATCH WRONG SIDES

Layer fabric so right sides face out and wrong sides face one another.

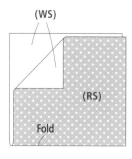

THREAD NEEDLE

Cutting thread on the diagonal makes it easier to pass through the eye of a needle. Using a threader makes the job even easier.

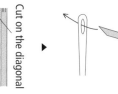

START SEWING

Pass the needle through fabric from 1–2, doubling back to sew over the same spot as shown (3–4). Sew once more over the same stitch before bringing the needle out two stitch lengths from the starting point to commence sewing.

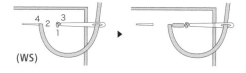

FINISH OFF

Double back to stitch as per below (1–2–3–4), then wind thread around the needle and pull needle through to form a knot. Sew back over last stitch again and clip thread.

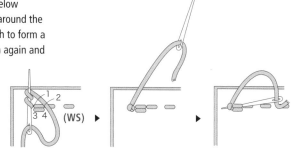

FOLD

The section of fabric created when fabric is folded over onto itself.

MAKING A KNOT

After threading the needle, make a knot at one of the ends of thread by winding it around your index finger and pulling thread through as shown.

Pull a few times

RUNNING STITCH

This stitch is the basis of hand sewing. Stitches are regular, of equal length and distance apart.

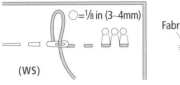 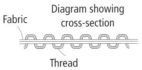

Guide needle in and out at regular intervals.

REVERSE RUNNING STITCH

A reverse stitch is made at every second to third stitch. This stitch is used where strong, sturdy sewing is required.

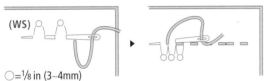

○ = ⅛ in (3~4mm)

1 Guide needle out every two-three stitches.
2 Go one stitch back, then guide the needle out two stitch lengths ahead.

HALF REVERSE STITCH

After making one stitch, bring needle back to create half a stitch length. Repeating this creates a sturdy line of stitching.

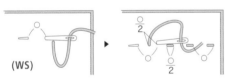

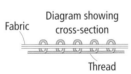

1 Make one stitch.
2 Go back half a stitch length and insert needle to create next stitch.

TRUE REVERSE STITCH

This is even stronger than the half-reverse stitch.

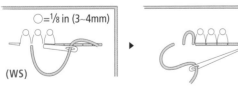

○ = ⅛ in (3~4mm)

1 Bring needle back to end of previous stitch then guide it through two stitch lengths ahead.
2 Pull thread through and repeat.

BAG STITCH

Use to finish off the seam on a bag created by folding one piece of material.

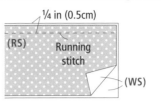 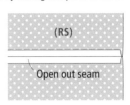

1 Match wrong sides and join using running stitch.

2 Open out seam with fingers.

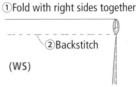

3 Turn seam edges in towards seam and sew to catch edges using back stitch.

4 Completed seam. Stitching cannot be seen from outside.

FRENCH SEAM

This is used to create casings or to open out a seam.

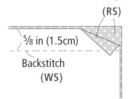

1 Match right sides and sew using stitch.

2 Open out seam with fingers.

3 Fold under each side of seam to about half the seam allowance and stitch down using running stitch.

4 Completed seam. Two rows of running stitch appear on the right side of material.

VERTICAL HEM STITCH

Use when attaching appliqué and so on. Stitches are made at right angles to the pieces of fabric being joined.

HEM STITCH

Match seam allowances of two pieces of fabric and, from right sides of fabric, make U shaped stitches along the fold line.

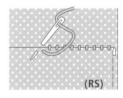 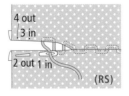

01. Contrasting Fabric Bag with Handles

Photo: page 4

● MATERIALS

Cable knit fabric (for outer fabric) 12 x 20 in
(30 x 50cm)

Tweed check (for outer gusset, lining fabric, inner
gusset) 28 x 20 in (70 x 50cm)

Striped tape for handles, set of two 1 in wide x
18 in (2.5cm wide x 45cm)

Fusible belt interfacing 1 in wide x 28 in (2.5cm
wide x 70cm)

Hand sewing thread such as MOCO brand, beige

Hand sewing thread such as Schappe Spun brand,
light brown

● USE FULL-SIZE PATTERN PIECE SIDE A

※ Measurements given in inches and centimeters

※○ Add figure in circle as seam allowance when
drafting pattern

(①cm = ³⁄₈ in)

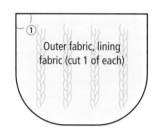

● INSTRUCTIONS

1 Apply fusible belt interfacing to lining and
gusset lining (use dry iron on medium heat)

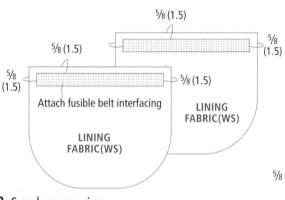

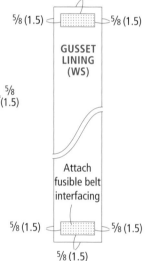

2 Sew outer fabric and gusset together

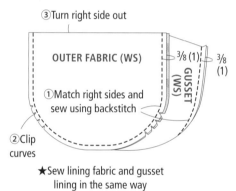

3 Sew bag opening

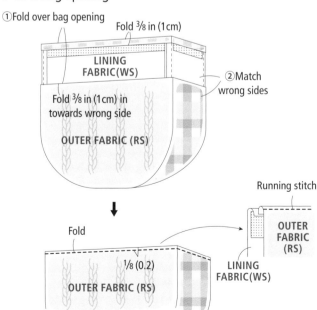

4 Attach handles

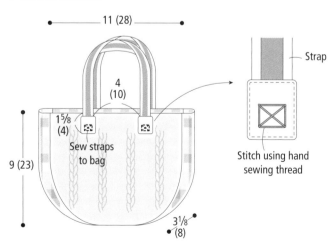

02. Lace Appliqué Bag with Handles

Photo: page 5

● MATERIALS

Tweed (for outer fabric and pocket) 34 x 18 in (85 x 45cm)

Printed fabric (for lining) 28 x 18 in (70 x 45cm)

Lace ⅜ in wide x 44 in (1cm wide x 110cm);
⅞ in wide x 8 in (2cm wide x 20cm)

Lace motifs 1⅛ in (3cm) diameter x 2
1⅝ in (4cm) diameter x 1

Hand sewing thread such as Schappe Spun brand, light yellow and brown

● USE FULL-SIZE PATTERN PIECE SIDE A

※ Measurements given in inches and centimeters

※○ Add figure in circle as seam allowance when drafting pattern
(①cm = ⅜ in)

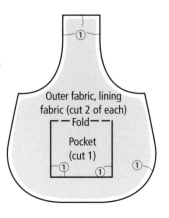

● INSTRUCTIONS

1 Create pocket and attach to bag

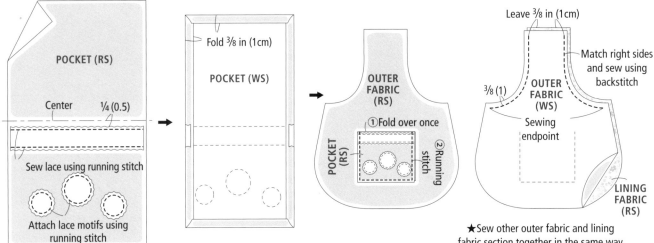

2 Match bag openings of outer fabric and lining fabric and sew together

★Sew other outer fabric and lining fabric section together in the same way

3 Sew outer fabric sections together and lining fabric sections together

4 Attach lace to bag opening

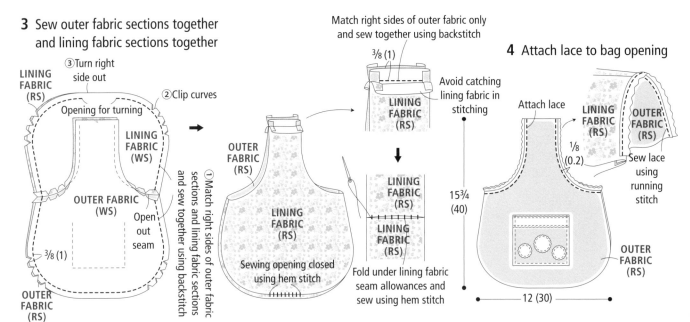

03. Two-way Bag

Photo: page 6

MATERIALS

Linen print (for bag) 18 x 38 in (45 x 95cm)
Ribbon (for handles) 1 in wide x 87 in (2.5cm
   wide x 220cm)
Fusible belt interfacing 1⅛ in wide x 32 in
   (3cm wide x 80cm)
Hand sewing thread such as MOCO brand,
   light purple
Hand sewing thread such as Schappe Spun brand,
   light beige

DRAFTING

※ Measurements given in inches and
   centimeters
※○ Add figure in circle as seam
   allowance when drafting pattern
   (⑮cm = ⅝ in; ⑤cm = 2 in)

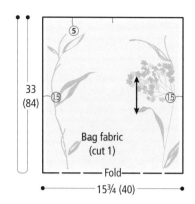

INSTRUCTIONS

1 Attach fusible belt interfacing
   (use dry iron on medium heat)

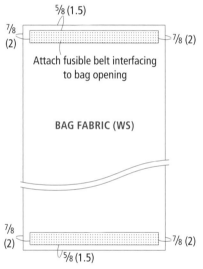

2 Sew sides of bag together

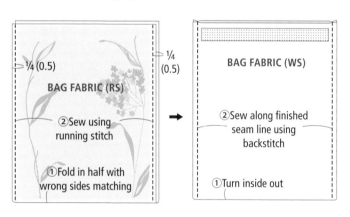

3 Fold ribbon for straps   **4** Sandwich straps between bag
                                  opening layers and attach

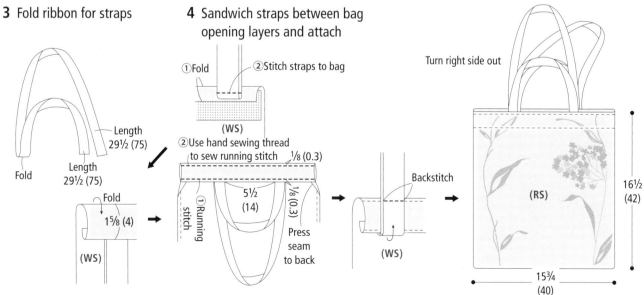

04. Checkout Basket Bag

Photo: page 7

● MATERIALS

Linen print (for bag, base, pocket) 38 x 36 in (95 x 90cm)

Voile (for drawstring section) 34 x 22 in (85 x 55cm)

Ribbon (for handles) 1 in wide x 85 in (2.5cm wide x 215cm)

Cord 1/8 in x 130 in (0.3cm thick x 330cm)

Snap fasteners 7/8 in (2cm) diameter x 2 sets

Hand sewing thread such as Schappe Spun brand, light beige, light blue

● DRAFTING

※ Measurements given in inches and centimeters

※○ Add figure in circle as seam allowance when drafting pattern
(①cm = 3/8 in; ⑮cm = 5/8 in; ②cm = 7/8 in; ③cm = 1 1/8 in; ④cm = 1 5/8 in)

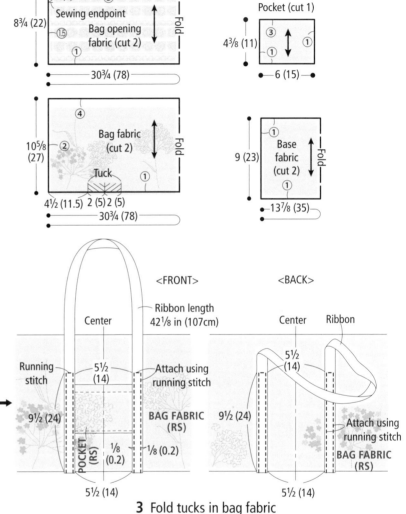

● INSTRUCTIONS

1 Attach pocket and ribbon (for handles)

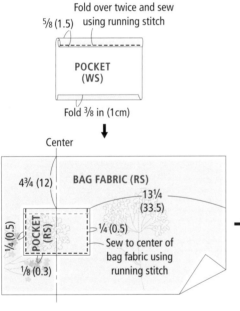

2 Sew sides of bag together

3 Fold tucks in bag fabric

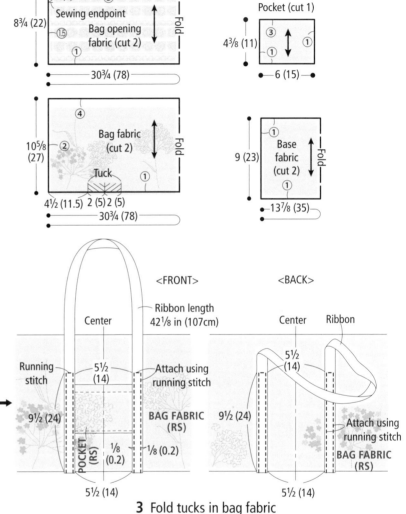

4 Sew bag and base together

BAG FABRIC (WS)

BASE FABRIC (WS)

Match right sides together and sew using backstitch

3/8 (1)

Clip all around seam allowance of bag fabric

BASE FABRIC (WS)

Fold over 3/8 in (1cm)

BASE FABRIC (RS)

② Fold seam allowance of other piece of base fabric

① Fold seam in towards base

③ Hem stitch outer sides of fabric together

5 Sew bag opening fabric

BAG OPENING FABRIC (RS)

3 1/8 (8) BAG OPENING FABRIC (WS) 3 1/8 (8)

Secure stitching here

5/8 (1.5)

Match right sides and stitch using backstitch

Backstitch

5/8 (1.5)

BAG OPENING FABRIC (RS)

BAG OPENING FABRIC (WS)

② Sew over end of stitching 2–3 times

① Fold each side of seam allowance under and sew through to outer side of fabric using running stitch (forming welt seams)

1/16 (0.1)

Fold over twice

7/8 (2)

(WS)

1/8 (0.2)   7/8 (2)

Cord casing

Cord casing

Fold over twice and sew using running stitch

BAG OPENING FABRIC (RS)

6 Sandwich bag opening fabric under opening of bag and sew

④ Turn out to right side

1 1/8 (3)

① Fold over opening of bag

② Sandwich bag opening fabric under and opening of bag and sew using running stitch

1/8 (0.2)

BAG OPENING FABRIC (RS)

Cord casing

BAG FABRIC (WS)

1 1/8 (3)

BAG OPENING FABRIC (RS)

③ Pass the cord through the casing

BAG FABRIC (WS)

Knot ends

Cord length 65 (165)

7 Attach snap fasteners

BAG OPENING FABRIC (RS)

8 1/8 (20.5)   8 1/8 (20.5)

Snap fastener (socket section)

Snap fastener (ball section)

Side

BAG FABRIC (RS)

Pocket side of bag

★ Attach snap fasteners to opposite side in the same way

● ATTACHING SNAP FASTENERS

1 out
4 in
2 in 3 out

Sew around snap fastener twice

30 3/4 (78)

BAG OPENING FABRIC (RS)

BAG FABRIC (RS)

18 (46)

9 (23)

14 (35)

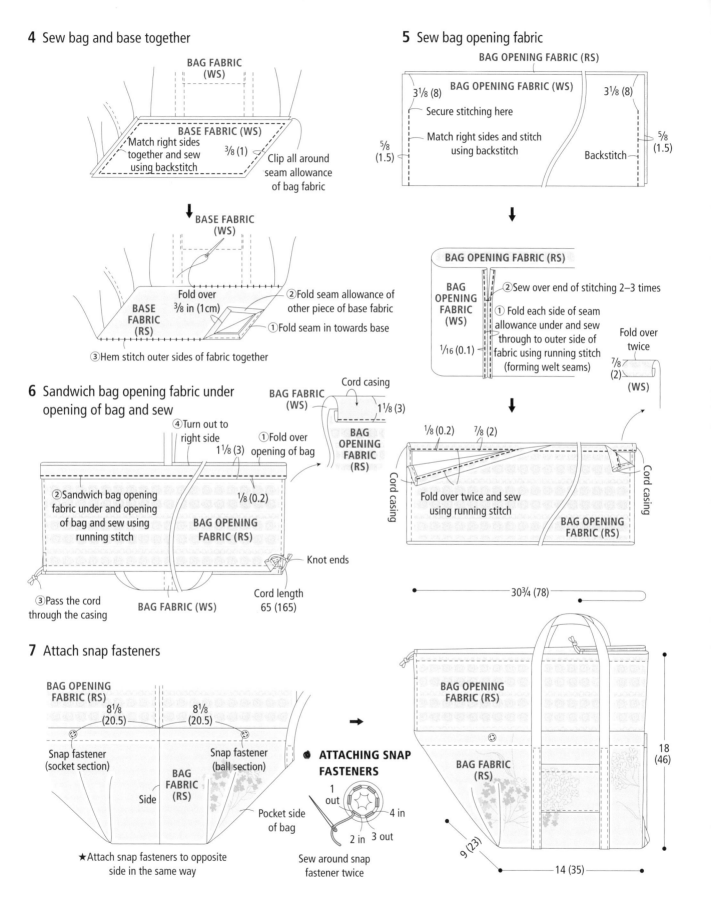

$o5. \sim 10.$ Eco Bag
Photo: pages 8–9

● MATERIALS FOR 5
Linen print (for bag, pocket) 46 x 24 in (115 x 60cm)
Button 7/8 in (2cm) diameter x 1
Hand sewing thread such as MOCO brand, beige
Hand sewing thread such as Schappe Spun brand,
bordeaux

● MATERIALS FOR 6
Linen gingham (for bag, pocket) 46 x 24 in
(115 x 60cm)
Button 7/8 in (2cm) diameter x 1
Tape-measure print tape 5/8 in wide x 8 in (1.5cm
wide x 20cm)
Hand sewing thread such as MOCO brand, red
Hand sewing thread such as Schappe Spun brand, red

● MATERIALS FOR 7
Checked linen (for bag, pocket) 50 x 24 in (125 x 60cm)
Button 7/8 x 7/8 in (2 x 2cm) square x 1
Alphabet print tape 5/8 in wide x 8 in (1.5cm wide x
20cm)
Hand sewing thread such as MOCO brand, red
Hand sewing thread such as Schappe Spun brand,
red

● MATERIALS FOR 8
Finely striped linen (for bag, pocket) 46 x 24 in
(115 x 60cm)
Button 7/8 x 7/8 in (2 x 2cm) square x 1
Polka dot print tape 5/8 in wide x 8 in (1.5cm wide
x 20cm)
Hand sewing thread such as MOCO brand, red
Hand sewing thread such as Schappe Spun brand,
red

● MATERIALS FOR 9
Striped linen (for bag, pocket) 50 x 24 in (125 x
60cm)
Button 7/8 in (2cm) diameter x 1
Hand sewing thread such as MOCO brand, red
Hand sewing thread such as Schappe Spun brand,
red

● MATERIALS FOR 10
Linen (for bag, pocket) 46 x 24 in (115 x 60cm)
Button 3/4 in (1.8cm) diameter x 1
Hand sewing thread such as MOCO brand, red
Hand sewing thread such as Schappe Spun brand,
red

● USE FULL-SIZE PATTERN PIECE SIDE A
※ Measurements given in inches and centimeters
※○ Add figure in circle as seam allowance when drafting pattern
(①cm = 3/8 in; ①⑤cm = 5/8 in; ②cm = 7/8 in; ④cm = 1 5/8 in)

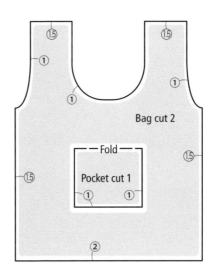

● INSTRUCTIONS

1 Create pocket

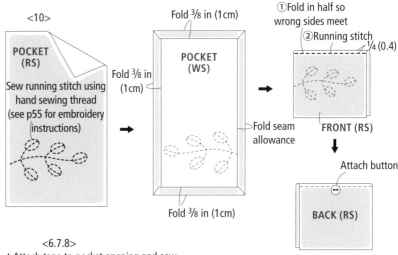

<6.7.8>
★Attach tape to pocket opening and sew
④Fold ends of tape under

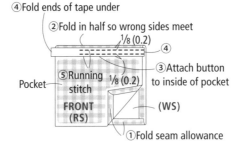

<5.9>
★Sew edge of pocket
without attaching tape

Attach button to inside of pocket

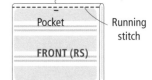

2 Attach pocket

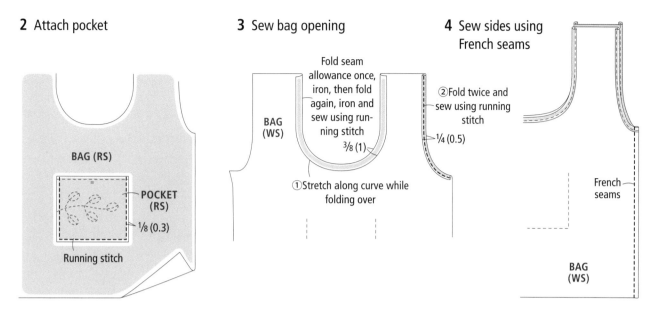

BAG (RS)

POCKET (RS)

1/8 (0.3)

Running stitch

3 Sew bag opening

Fold seam allowance once, iron, then fold again, iron and sew using running stitch 3/8 (1)

BAG (WS)

①Stretch along curve while folding over

②Fold twice and sew using running stitch

1/4 (0.5)

4 Sew sides using French seams

French seams

BAG (WS)

5 Fold gussets in base and sew

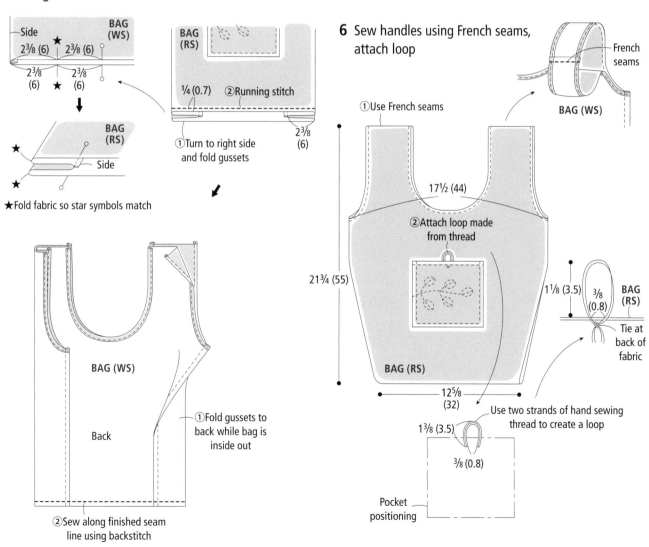

Side

BAG (WS)

2 3/8 (6) 2 3/8 (6)

2 3/8 (6) 2 3/8 (6)

★

★

BAG (RS)

★

Side

★

★Fold fabric so star symbols match

BAG (RS)

1/4 (0.7) ②Running stitch

①Turn to right side and fold gussets

2 3/8 (6)

BAG (WS)

Back

①Fold gussets to back while bag is inside out

②Sew along finished seam line using backstitch

6 Sew handles using French seams, attach loop

French seams

BAG (WS)

①Use French seams

17 1/2 (44)

②Attach loop made from thread

21 3/4 (55)

BAG (RS)

12 5/8 (32)

1 1/8 (3.5) 3/8 (0.8) BAG (RS)

Tie at back of fabric

Use two strands of hand sewing thread to create a loop

1 3/8 (3.5)

3/8 (0.8)

Pocket positioning

11. Reversible Full-circle Bag

Photo: pages 10–11

● MATERIALS

Printed fabric (for outer fabric, casing, strap guard)
  44 x 36 in (110 x 90cm)
Dobby fabric (for lining) 30 x 30 in (75 x 75cm)
Cord for strap ⅜ in thick x 71 in (1cm thick x 180cm)
Hand sewing thread such as MOCO brand, blue
Hand sewing thread such as Schappe Spun brand,
  light blue

● MATERIALS FOR MAKING CORD CARRIERS

Plain fabric 32 x 32 in (80 x 80cm)
Cord ⅜ in thick x 71 (1cm thick x 180cm)

● USE FULL-SIZE PATTERN PIECE SIDE B

※ Measurements given in inches and centimeters
※○ Add figure in circle as seam allowance when
  drafting pattern
  (①cm = ⅜ in)

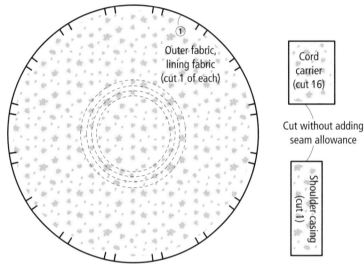

Outer fabric,
lining fabric
(cut 1 of each)

Cord
carrier
(cut 16)

Cut without adding
seam allowance

Shoulder casing
(cut 1)

● INSTRUCTIONS

1 Sew cord carriers

2 Sew outer fabric and lining fabric together

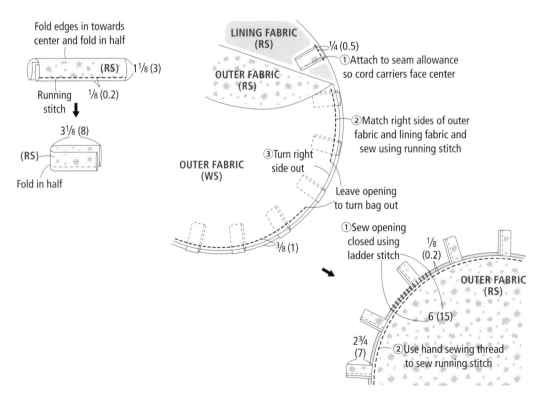

Fold edges in towards
center and fold in half

(RS) 1⅛ (3)

Running
stitch

⅛ (0.2)

3⅛ (8)

(RS)

Fold in half

LINING FABRIC
(RS)

OUTER FABRIC
(RS)

¼ (0.5)

①Attach to seam allowance
so cord carriers face center

②Match right sides of outer
fabric and lining fabric and
sew using running stitch

③Turn right
side out

OUTER FABRIC
(WS)

Leave opening
to turn bag out

⅜ (1)

①Sew opening
closed using
ladder stitch

⅛
(0.2)

OUTER FABRIC
(RS)

6 (15)

2¾
(7)

②Use hand sewing thread
to sew running stitch

3 Stitch base

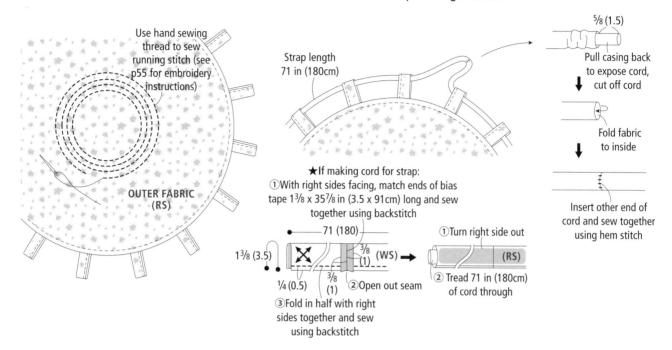

Use hand sewing thread to sew running stitch (see p55 for embroidery instructions)

OUTER FABRIC (RS)

4 Thread cord for straps through carriers

Strap length 71 in (180cm)

⅝ (1.5)

Pull casing back to expose cord, cut off cord

Fold fabric to inside

Insert other end of cord and sew together using hem stitch

★If making cord for strap:
①With right sides facing, match ends of bias tape 1⅜ x 35⅞ in (3.5 x 91cm) long and sew together using backstitch

1⅜ (3.5)

71 (180)

⅜ (1)

¼ (0.5)

⅜ (1)

(WS)

②Open out seam

③Fold in half with right sides together and sew using backstitch

①Turn right side out

(RS)

② Tread 71 in (180cm) of cord through

5 Attach shoulder casing

①Fold twice and sew using running stitch

⅜ (1)

SHOULDER CASING (WS)

⅜ (1)

② Fold ⅜ in (1cm)

(RS)

Loop

Encase both straps and stitch shoulder casing using running stitch

28⅜ (72)

Shoulder casing

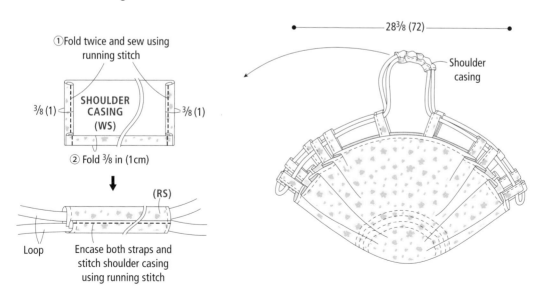

12. Reversible Puff-out Tuck Bag

Photo: pages 10–11

● MATERIALS

Printed fabric (for outer fabric, outer handle fabric, cord) 30 x 34 in (75 x 85cm)

Dobby fabric (for lining, inner handle fabric) 28 x 34 in (70 x 85cm)

Hand sewing thread such as MOCO brand, blue

Hand sewing thread such as Schappe Spun brand, light blue

● USE FULL-SIZE PATTERN PIECE SIDE A

※ Measurements given in inches and centimeters

※○ Add figure in circle as seam allowance when drafting pattern

(①cm = 3/8 in; ③cm = 1 1/8 in)

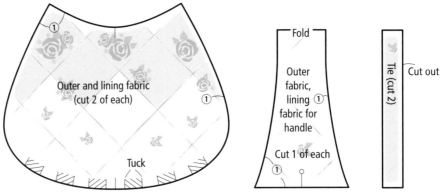

● INSTRUCTIONS

1 Create tucks in outer and lining parts of bag

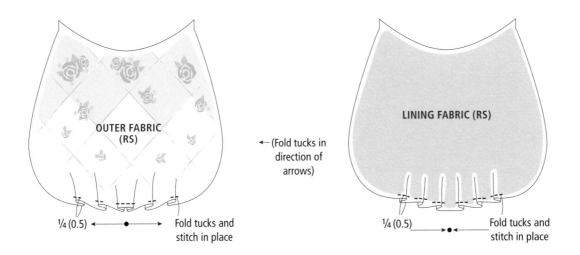

← (Fold tucks in direction of arrows)

2 Openings of bag for outer and lining fabrics

★ Fold lining fabric in the same way

3 Match outer fabric and lining fabric and sew together

Sew outer and lining fabrics using backstitch

LINING FABRIC (WS)

OUTER FABRIC (WS)

③ Sew outer and lining fabrics separately for sections left open

⑤ Turn to right side through outer fabric

③

Leave 7/8 in (2cm)

Leave 7/8 in (2cm)

OUTER FABRIC (WS)

3/8 (1)

3/8 (1)

② Sew outer fabric and lining together using backstitch

④ Clip curves

① Match outer and lining sections

Fold 3/8 in (1cm)　　TIE (WS)

3/8 (1)　　　　　TIE (RS)

Fold edges to center, fold in half and sew

4 Sew strap and ties

3/8 (1)　　② Clip curves

① Match right sides of outer and lining pieces for strap and sew using backstitch

STRAP (WS)

③ Turn right side out

STRAP (RS)

3/8 (1)

1/8 (0.2)

Use hand sewing thread to sew running stitches (see p55 on how to create running stitches)

STRAP (RS)

5 Sew bag opening

STRAP (RS)

1/4 (0.5)

Use running stitch to sew strap to seam allowance of lining (sew ties to lining in the same way)

OUTER FABRIC (RS)

Side

LINING FABRIC (WS)

11 5/8 (29.5)

Sandwich tie between layers

Sandwich strap between layers on sides of bag

1/8 (0.2)

Use hand sewing thread to sew running stitches

(RS)

13 1/2 (34)

19 3/8 (49)

$3o. \sim 38$, Little Fancy Purse in Soft Fabric

Photo: pages 22–23

● **USE FULL-SIZE PATTERN PIECE SIDE A**

※For materials needed for Bag 31 and instructions for bags 30–38, see p36–37

Bag no	Outer fabric	Lining fabric	Decoration for Bag	Material for ties 36 in (90cm) excluding Bag 33	Decoration for Ties
30	print [18 x 10 in (45 × 25cm)]	linen [18 x 10 in (45 × 25cm)]		satin ribbon [¼ in (0.5cm) wide]	fabric yo-yos [1⅞ in (4.5cm) diameter x 4]
32	print for both outer and lining fabric [34 x 10 in (85 × 25cm)]	print for both outer (cut from main fabric)		ribbon [¼ in (0.5cm) wide]	simple knot
33	stripe for both outer and lining fabric [34 x 10 in (85 × 25cm)]	stripe [(cut from main fabric)]		cord [⅛ in thick x 40 in (0.3 x 100cm)]	wooden beads [10mm diameter x 4]
34	double gauze for both outer and lining fabric [34 x 10 in (85 × 25cm)]	double gauze	French knot stitch (silk thread in pink)	gauze ribbon [⅜ in (0.8cm) wide]	ball made from outer fabric [1⅜ in (3.5cm) diameter circle of fabric x 2, cotton wool]
35	linen for both outer and lining fabric [34 x 10 in (85 × 25cm)]	linen	lazy daisy stitch, French knot stitch (silk thread in pink)	lace [¼ in (0.6cm) wide]	glass bead [10mm diameter]
36	linen for both outer and lining fabric [34 x 10 in (85 × 25cm)]	linen	double cross stitch (silk thread in purple, chartreuse, light blue) organza frill ribbon ⅜ in wide x 18 in (1 x 45cm)	crochet chain (silk thread in purple, crochet hook size 4/0)	wooden beads [15mm diameter x 2]
37	check [18 x 10 in (45 × 25cm)]	linen [18 x 10 in (45 × 25cm)]		rope ¼ in (0.5cm) thick]	ball made from outer fabric [1⅞ in (4.5cm) diameter circle of fabric x 2, cotton wool]
38	print [14 x 20 in (35 × 50cm)]	linen [18 x 10 in (45 × 25cm)]		outer fabric [cut 2, 1½ ×18 in (3 x 45cm)]: fold edges to center, fold in half and sew using running stitch	buttons [½ in (1.2cm) diameter x 4]

※Silk thread colors are gradated

● **USE FULL-SIZE PATTERN PIECE SIDE A**

※ Measurements given in inches and centimeters

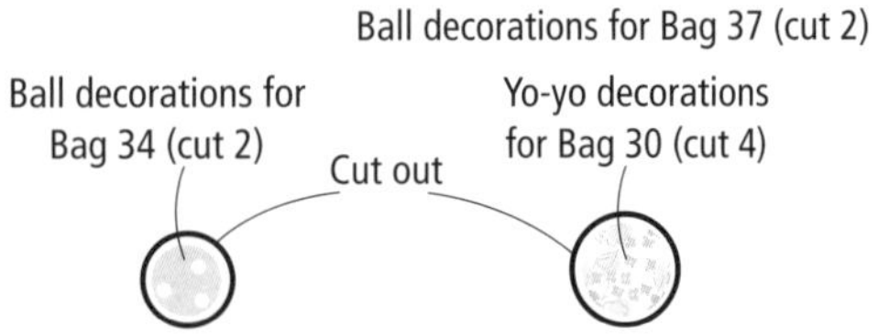

Ball decorations for Bag 37 (cut 2)

Ball decorations for Bag 34 (cut 2)   Cut out   Yo-yo decorations for Bag 30 (cut 4)

Cut out   Tie for Bag 38 (cut 2)
Fold

● **HOW TO MAKE TIES**

<38>   <36>

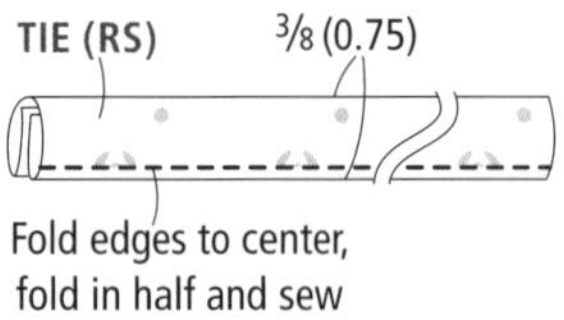

TIE (RS)   ⅜ (0.75)

Fold edges to center, fold in half and sew

Create crochet chain from 79 in (2m) of silk thread (3 strands)

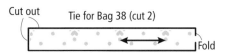

★Create two 18 in (45cm)-long chains

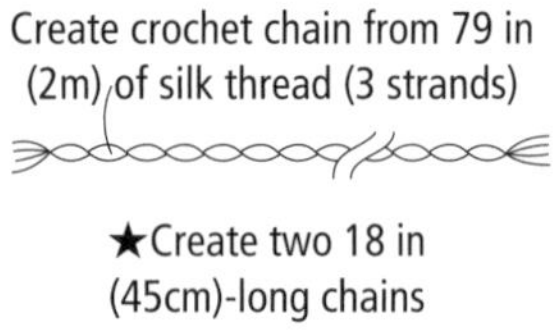

● HOW TO MAKE BALL DECORATIONS

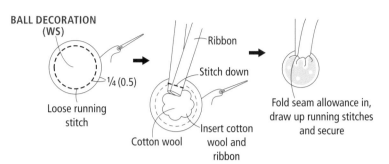

● HOW TO MAKE YO-YOS

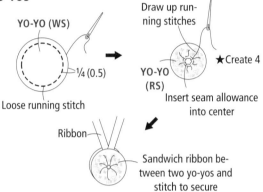

● FULL SIZE EMBROIDERY DIAGRAM FOR BAG 36

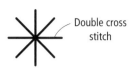

Double cross stitch

● FULL SIZE EMBROIDERY DIAGRAM FOR BAG 35

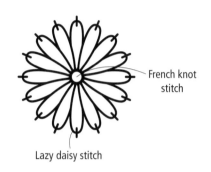

French knot stitch

Lazy daisy stitch

● HOW TO MAKE EMBROIDERY STITCHES

● FOR LAZY DAISY STITCH AND DOUBLE CROSS STITCH, SEE PAGE 37

Lazy daisy stitch	French knot stitch
3 out / 2 in / 1 Out — 4 in / 3 / 2 1	1 out / 2 in / 1 — A Wind around — B Wind around again
Running stitch	**Outline stitch**
3 out 2 in 1 out — 5 out 4 in 3 2 1 — - - -	3 out / 1 out 2 in — 3 5 out / 1 2 4 in — Repeat 2–3
Outline stitch	**Cross stitch**
2 in / 3 out / 1 out — 2 4 in / 3 5 out / 1 — |||||	1 Out / 3 out 2 in — 4 in / 3 Out — X

Shoulder Bag with Flaps (S, L)

Photo: page 13

● MATERIALS FOR 15

Print fabric (for outer fabric) 16 x 38 in (40 x 95cm)

Double layer gauze (for lining, shoulder strap, button loop) 24 x 40 in (60 x 100cm)

Buttons 1⅛ in (2.7cm) diameter x 2

Fusible interfacing for strap...finished measurements of tape 1 in wide x 40 in (2.5cm wide x 100cm)

Hand sewing thread such as MOCO brand, green

Hand sewing thread such as Schappe Spun brand, chartreuse

● MATERIALS FOR 16

Print fabric (for outer fabric) 10 x 28 in (25 x 70cm)

Double layer gauze (for lining, shoulder strap, button loop) 14 x 40 in (35 x 100cm)

Button ⅞ in (2.2cm) diameter x 1

Fusible interfacing for strap... finished measurements of tape 1 in wide x 40 in (2.5cm wide x 100cm)

Hand sewing thread such as MOCO brand, green

Hand sewing thread such as Schappe Spun brand, chart

※ Measurements given in inches and centimeters
※○ Add figure in circle as seam allowance when drafting pattern
(①cm = ⅜ in)

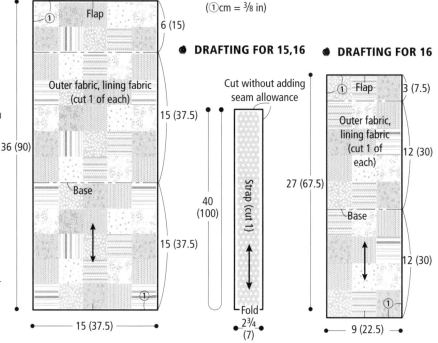

● DRAFTING FOR 15

Flap

① 6 (15)

Outer fabric, lining fabric (cut 1 of each)

15 (37.5)

36 (90)

Base

15 (37.5)

15 (37.5)

① ①

● DRAFTING FOR 15,16

Cut without adding seam allowance

Strap (cut 1)

40 (100)

Fold

2¾ (7)

● DRAFTING FOR 16

① Flap

3 (7.5)

Outer fabric, lining fabric (cut 1 of each)

12 (30)

27 (67.5)

Base

12 (30)

① ①

9 (22.5)

● INSTRUCTIONS FOR 15,16

1 Sew outer fabric and lining fabric together

<16>

LINING FABRIC (RS)

OUTER FABRIC (WS)

①Sandwich loop between layers

loop (cut 2 for Bag 15) (cut 1 for Bag 16)

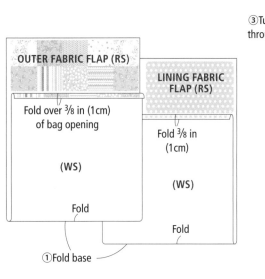

OUTER FABRIC FLAP (RS)

LINING FABRIC FLAP (RS)

Fold over ⅜ in (1cm) of bag opening

Fold ⅜ in (1cm)

(WS)

(WS)

Fold

Fold

①Fold base

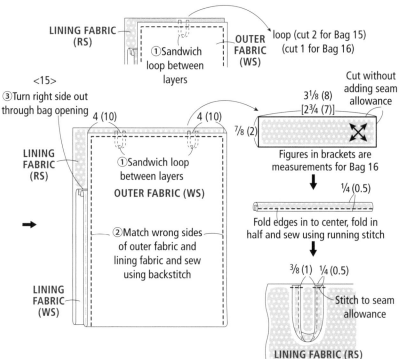

<15>

③Turn right side out through bag opening

4 (10)

4 (10)

LINING FABRIC (RS)

①Sandwich loop between layers

OUTER FABRIC (WS)

②Match wrong sides of outer fabric and lining fabric and sew using backstitch

LINING FABRIC (WS)

Cut without adding seam allowance

3⅛ (8)
[2¾ (7)]

⅞ (2)

Figures in brackets are measurements for Bag 16

¼ (0.5)

Fold edges in to center, fold in half and sew using running stitch

⅜ (1) ¼ (0.5)

Stitch to seam allowance

LINING FABRIC (RS)

2 Sew bag opening and flap

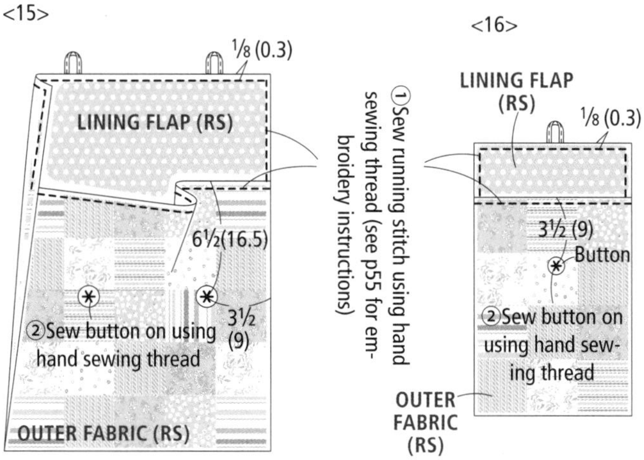

<15>
1/8 (0.3)
LINING FLAP (RS)
6½(16.5)
3½ (9)
②Sew button on using hand sewing thread
OUTER FABRIC (RS)
①Sew running stitch using hand sewing thread (see p55 for embroidery instructions)
<16>
LINING FLAP (RS)
1/8 (0.3)
3½ (9)
Button
②Sew button on using hand sewing thread
OUTER FABRIC (RS)

3 Sew strap

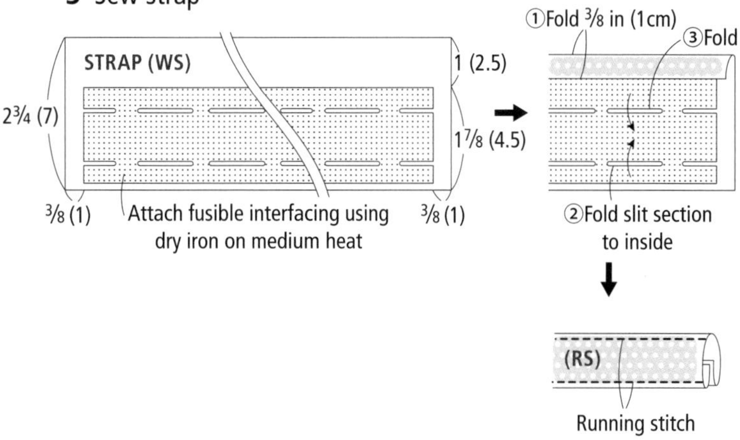

STRAP (WS)
1 (2.5)
2¾ (7)
1⅞ (4.5)
⅜ (1)
Attach fusible interfacing using dry iron on medium heat
⅜ (1)
①Fold ⅜ in (1cm)
③Fold
②Fold slit section to inside
(RS)
Running stitch

4 Attach strap

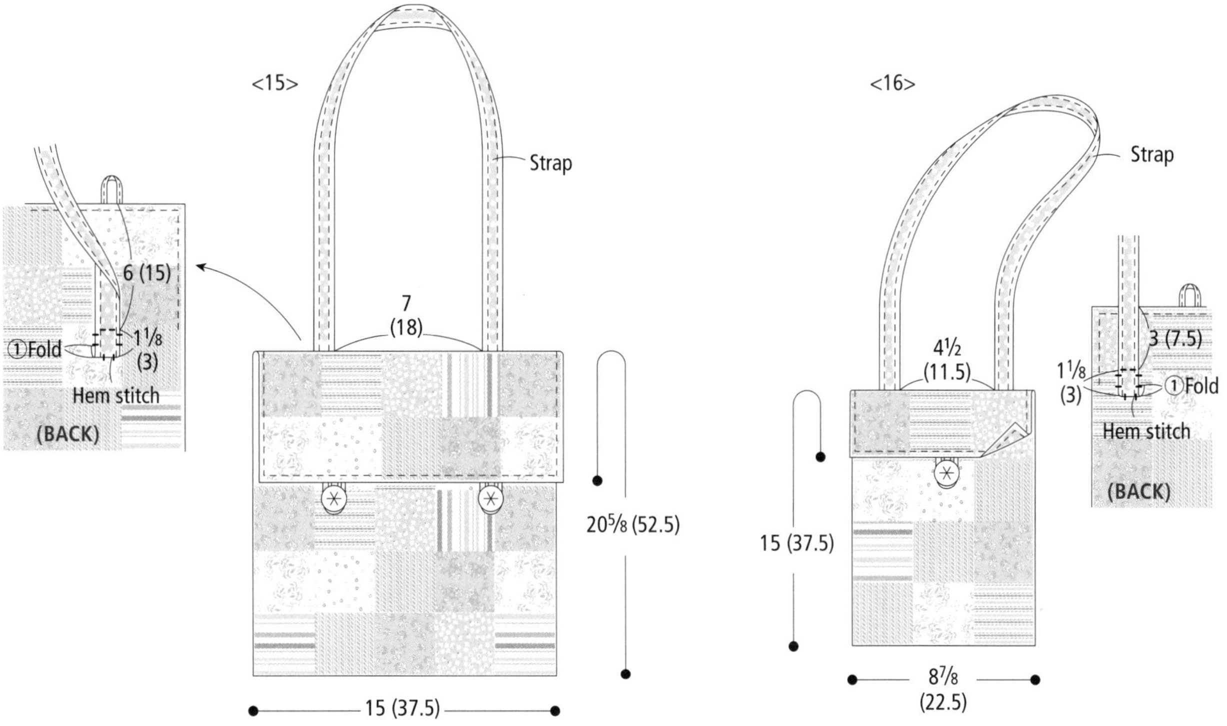

<15>
6 (15)
①Fold
1⅛ (3)
Hem stitch
(BACK)
Strap
7 (18)
20⅝ (52.5)
15 (37.5)
<16>
Strap
4½ (11.5)
3 (7.5)
1⅛ (3)
①Fold
Hem stitch
(BACK)
15 (37.5)
8⅞ (22.5)

13, 14. Little Purse with Flaps (S, L)

Photo: page 12

● MATERIALS FOR 13

Print fabric (for outer fabric) 8 x 16 in (20 x 40cm)
Double layer gauze (for lining, button loop)
  8 x 16 in (20 x 40cm)
Button 7/8 in (2.2cm) diameter x 1
Hand sewing thread such as MOCO brand, green
Hand sewing thread such as Schappe Spun brand,
  chartreuse

● MATERIALS FOR 14

Print fabric (for outer fabric) 8 x 22 in (20 x 55cm)
Double layer gauze (for lining) 8 x 22 in (20 x 55cm)
Button 7/8 in (2.2cm) x 1
Hand sewing thread such as MOCO brand, green
Hand sewing thread such as Schappe Spun brand,
  chartreuse

● DRAFTING FOR 13, 14

※ Measurements given in inches
  and centimeters
※○ Add figure in circle as seam
  allowance when drafting pattern
  (①cm = 3/8 in)

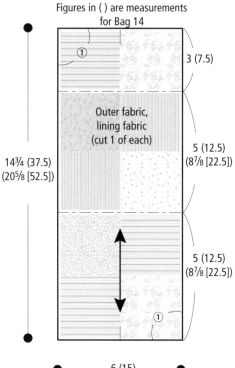

Figures in ( ) are measurements for Bag 14

①

3 (7.5)

Outer fabric, lining fabric (cut 1 of each)

14¾ (37.5)
(20⅝ [52.5])

5 (12.5)
(8⅞ [22.5])

5 (12.5)
(8⅞ [22.5])

①

6 (15)

● INSTRUCTIONS FOR 13,14

※REFER TO STEPS 1 AND 2 FOR BAGS 15, 16

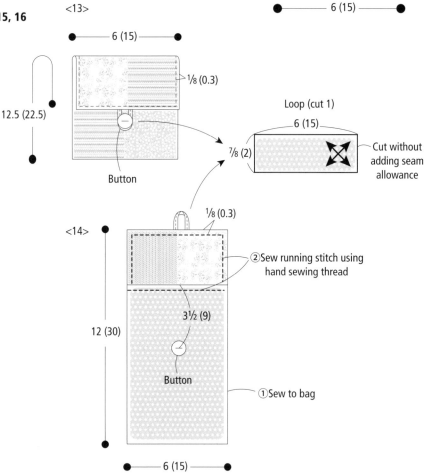

<13>

6 (15)

12.5 (22.5)

1/8 (0.3)

Button

Loop (cut 1)

6 (15)

7/8 (2)

Cut without adding seam allowance

<14>

1/8 (0.3)

② Sew running stitch using hand sewing thread

3½ (9)

Button

12 (30)

① Sew to bag

6 (15)

21. Long Tote with Floral Motifs
Photo: page 16

● MATERIALS
Corduroy (for outer fabric) 20 x 24 in (50 x 60cm)
Plain fabric (for lining, base board fabric) 22 x 20 in
   (55 x 50cm)
Fusible wadding (medium weight) 18 x 20 in (45 x 50cm)
Poly fiber wadding (for base board) 4 x 14 in (10 x 35cm)
Handle with flower motifs 23 in (58cm) x 1
Flower button ⅞ in (2.2cm) diameter x 1
Hand sewing thread such as MOCO brand, gradated pale
   blue tones
Hand sewing thread such as Schappe Spun brand, beige

● DRAFTING
※ Measurements given in inches and centimeters
※○ Add figure in circle as seam allowance when drafting pattern
   (①cm = ⅜ in; ⑮cm = ⅝ in; ⑤cm = 2 in)

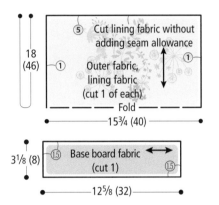

※ Cut outer fabric to 18 x 23⅝ in
   (46 × 60cm)
※ Cut fusible quilt wadding to
   15¾ x 18 in (40 × 46cm)

● INSTRUCTIONS

1 Attach fusible wadding to outer fabric
(use a dry iron on medium setting)

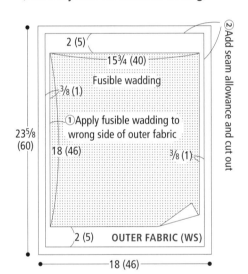

2 Sew outer section and lining together

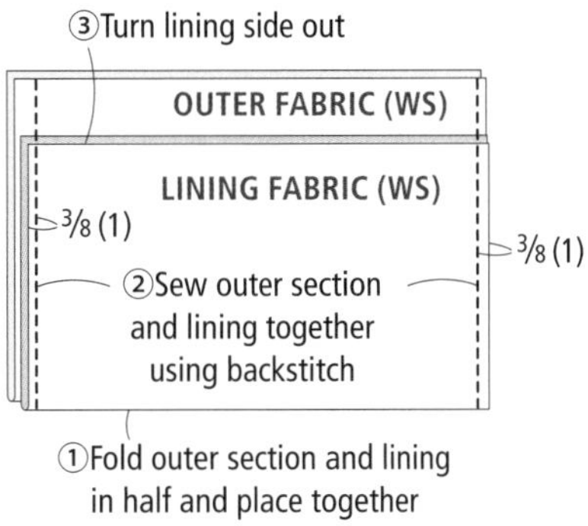

③ Turn lining side out
OUTER FABRIC (WS)
LINING FABRIC (WS)
⅜ (1)   ⅜ (1)
② Sew outer section
and lining together
using backstitch
① Fold outer section and lining
in half and place together

3 Sew gussets on base

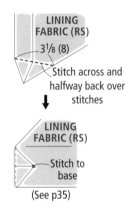

LINING FABRIC (RS)
3⅛ (8)
Stitch across and
halfway back over
stitches

LINING FABRIC (RS)
Stitch to base
(See p35)

● KNOT TO FINISH

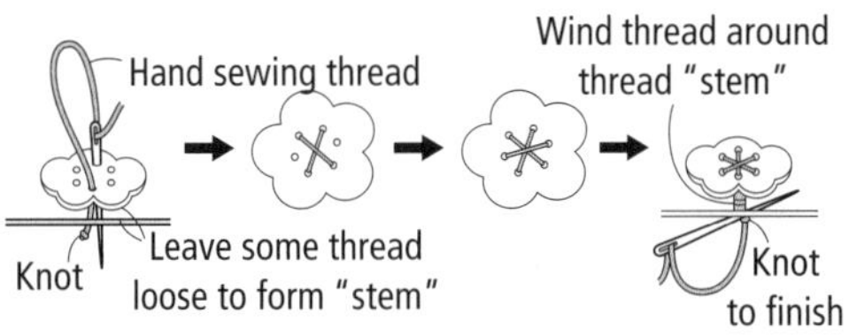

Hand sewing thread
Wind thread around thread "stem"
Knot   Leave some thread loose to form "stem"
Knot to finish

4 Create loop and attach to bag

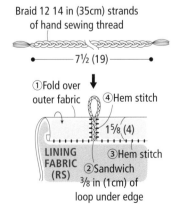

Braid 12 14 in (35cm) strands
of hand sewing thread
7½ (19)

① Fold over outer fabric
④ Hem stitch
1⅝ (4)
LINING FABRIC (RS)
③ Hem stitch
② Sandwich
⅜ in (1cm) of
loop under edge

5 Attach straps and button

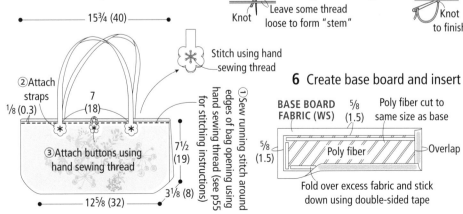

15¾ (40)
② Attach straps
⅛ (0.3)
7 (18)
③ Attach buttons using hand sewing thread
Stitch using hand sewing thread
① Sew running stitch around edges of bag opening using hand sewing thread (see p55 for stitching instructions)
7½ (19)
12⅝ (32)
3⅛ (8)

6 Create base board and insert

BASE BOARD FABRIC (WS)
⅝ (1.5)
Poly fiber cut to same size as base
⅝ (1.5)
Poly fiber
Overlap
Fold over excess fabric and stick down using double-sided tape

22. Tote with Pompom

Photo: page 17

● MATERIALS

Felt (for bag, base board fabric) 16 x 22 in (40 x 55cm)

Poly fiber wadding (for base board) 2 x 12 in (5 x 30cm)

Wool for pompom

Hand sewing thread such as MOCO brand, gradated orange tones

Hand sewing thread such as Schappe Spun brand, light brown

Crochet hook 8mm

Double sided tape

● DRAFTING

※ Measurements given in inches and centimeters

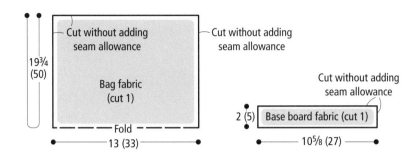

Cut without adding seam allowance

Cut without adding seam allowance

Cut without adding seam allowance

19¾ (50)

Bag fabric (cut 1)

Fold

13 (33)

2 (5)

Base board fabric (cut 1)

10⅝ (27)

● INSTRUCTIONS

1 Sew both sides

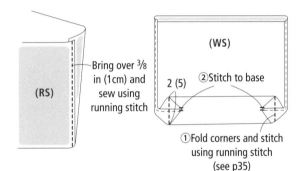

(RS)

Bring over ⅜ in (1cm) and sew using running stitch

2 Sew gussets for base

(WS)

②Stitch to base

2 (5)

①Fold corners and stitch using running stitch (see p35)

3 Sew around bag opening

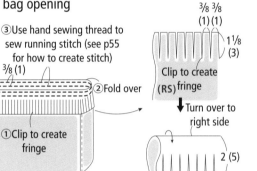

③Use hand sewing thread to sew running stitch (see p55 for how to create stitch)

¼ (0.5) ⅜ (1)

②Fold over

(RS)

①Clip to create fringe

⅜ ⅜ (1) (1)

1⅛ (3)

(RS) Clip to create fringe

Turn over to right side

2 (5)

(RS)

4 Create handles

★Make two

Crochet chain from three strands of wool

15¾ (40)

5 Create pompom

2⅜ (6)

Wind wool around card 85 times

Thick card

Remove from card and tie around center

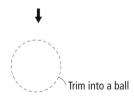

Trim into a ball

6 Attach handles and pompom

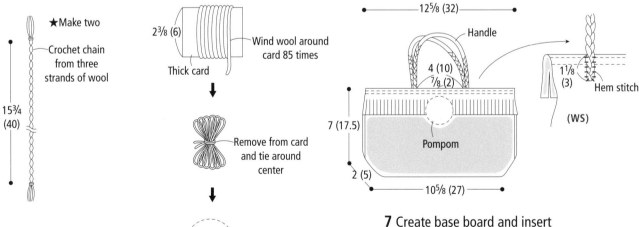

12⅝ (32)

Handle

4 (10)

⅞ (2)

7 (17.5)

Pompom

2 (5)

10⅝ (27)

1⅛ (3)

Hem stitch

(WS)

7 Create base board and insert

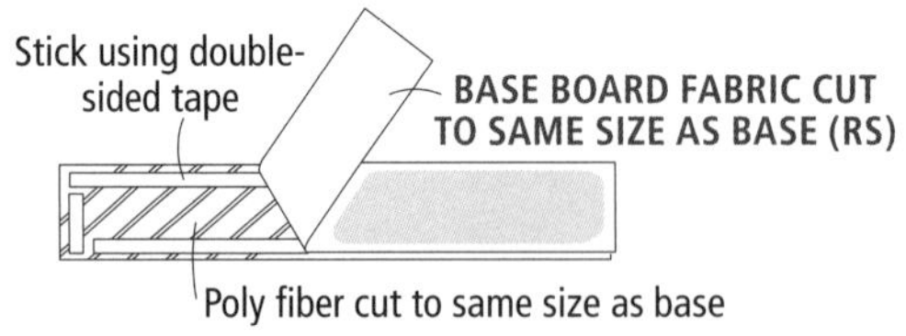

Stick using double-sided tape

BASE BOARD FABRIC CUT TO SAME SIZE AS BASE (RS)

Poly fiber cut to same size as base

23. ~ 25. Picnic Tote

Photo: pages 18–19

● MATERIALS FOR 23

Linen gingham (for outer fabric) 20 x 32 in (50 x 80cm)
Linen (for lining, base board fabric) 30 x 32 in (75 x 80cm)
Poly fiber wadding (for base board) 8 x 10 in (20 x 25cm)
Fusible belt interfacing 1⅛ in wide x 36 in (3cm wide x 90cm)
Punched leather tape (for handles) ⅝ in wide x 40 in
    (1.5cm wide x 100cm)
Hand sewing thread such as MOCO brand, blue
Hand sewing thread such as Schappe Spun brand, white

● MATERIALS FOR 24

Printed fabric (for outer fabric) 44 in wide x 16 in (110cm
    wide x 40cm)
Linen (for lining, base board fabric) 24 x 26 in (60 x 65cm)
Poly fiber wadding (for base board) 8 x 8 in (20 x 20cm)
Fusible belt interfacing 1⅛ in wide x 28 in (3cm wide x 70cm)
Punched leather tape (for handles) ⅝ in wide x 36 in
    (1.5cm wide x 90cm)
Hand sewing thread such as MOCO brand, blue
Hand sewing thread such as Schappe Spun brand, white

● MATERIALS FOR 25

Linen (for outer fabric) 14 x 20 in (35 x 50cm)
Linen (for lining, base board fabric) 20 x 20 in (50 x 50cm)
Printed fabric (for appliqué) 4 x 4 in (10 x 10cm)
Lace ⅜ in wide x 24 (1cm wide x 60cm)
Heat-bondable double sided sheet
Poly fiber wadding (for base board) 6 x 6 in (15 x 15cm)
Fusible belt interfacing 1⅛ in wide x 22 in (3cm wide x 55cm)
Punched leather tape (for handles) ⅝ in wide x 24 in
    (1.5cm wide x 60cm)
Hand sewing thread such as MOCO brand, gradated pale
    blue tones
Hand sewing thread such as Schappe Spun brand, beige

● MATERIALS FOR ALL PICNIC TOTES

Magnet fasteners (sew-on type) x 1
Double sided tape

※ Measurements given in inches and
    centimeters
※○ Add figure in circle as seam
    allowance when drafting pattern
    (①cm = ⅜ in; ⑮cm = ⅝ in)

● DRAFTING FOR BAG 24

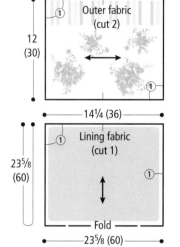

① Outer fabric (cut 2)
12 (30)
14¼ (36)

① Lining fabric (cut 1)
23⅝ (60)
Fold
23⅝ (60)

● DRAFTING FOR BAG 23

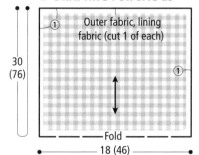

① Outer fabric, lining fabric (cut 1 of each)
30 (76)
Fold
18 (46)

● DRAFTING FOR BAG 25

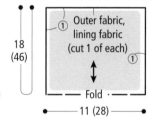

① Outer fabric, lining fabric (cut 1 of each)
18 (46)
Fold
11 (28)

● DRAFTING FOR BAGS 23, 24, 25

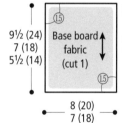

⑮ Base board fabric (cut 1)
9½ (24)
7 (18)
5½ (14)
⑮
8 (20)
7 (18)
5½ (14)

Measurements listed from top to bottom to correspond to bags 23, 24, 25

● INSTRUCTIONS

1 Sew outer fabric

★Attach appliqué to outer fabric

<25>

⅝ (1.5)
3 (7.5)
Sew around appliqué using blanket stitch (see p55 for how to make stitches)
Sew lace using running stitch
OUTER FABRIC (RS)
⅝ (1.5)

● CREATE APPLIQUÉ

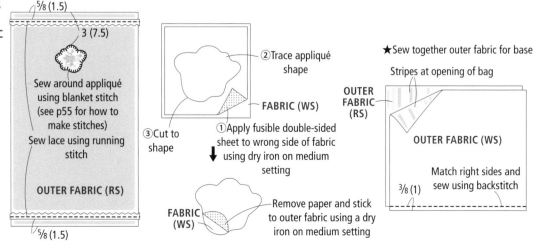

②Trace appliqué shape
FABRIC (WS)
③Cut to shape
①Apply fusible double-sided sheet to wrong side of fabric using dry iron on medium setting
FABRIC (WS)
Remove paper and stick to outer fabric using a dry iron on medium setting

★Sew together outer fabric for base
Stripes at opening of bag
OUTER FABRIC (RS)
OUTER FABRIC (WS)
Match right sides and sew using backstitch
⅜ (1)

2 Attach fusible belt interfacing to lining fabric using a dry iron on medium setting

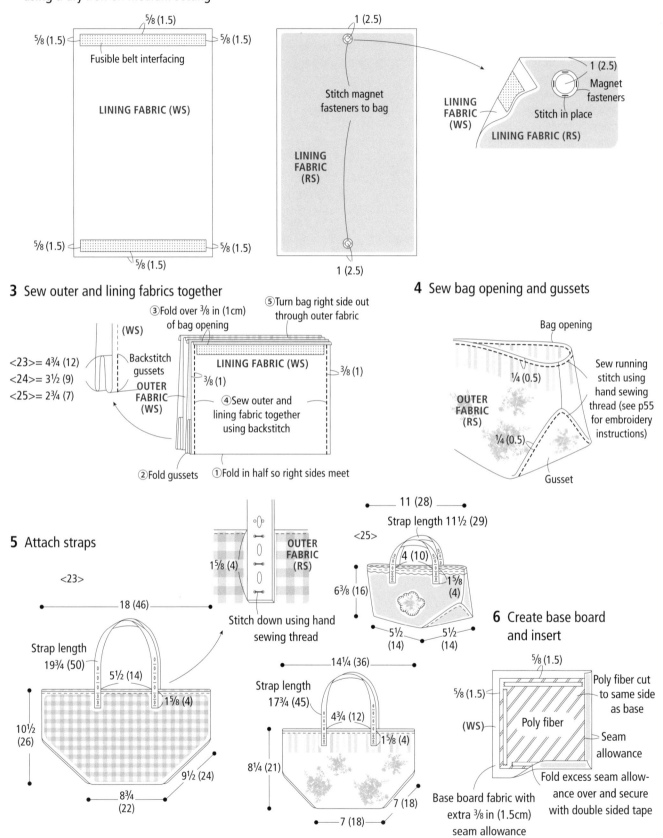

⁵⁄₈ (1.5)
⁵⁄₈ (1.5)
⁵⁄₈ (1.5)
Fusible belt interfacing

LINING FABRIC (WS)

⁵⁄₈ (1.5)
⁵⁄₈ (1.5)
⁵⁄₈ (1.5)

1 (2.5)
Stitch magnet fasteners to bag

LINING FABRIC (RS)

1 (2.5)

LINING FABRIC (WS)

1 (2.5)
Magnet fasteners
Stitch in place
LINING FABRIC (RS)

3 Sew outer and lining fabrics together

③Fold over ³⁄₈ in (1cm) of bag opening
⑤Turn bag right side out through outer fabric

(WS)

<23>= 4¾ (12)
<24>= 3½ (9)
<25>= 2¾ (7)

Backstitch gussets
OUTER FABRIC (WS)

LINING FABRIC (WS)
³⁄₈ (1)
³⁄₈ (1)
④Sew outer and lining fabric together using backstitch

②Fold gussets
①Fold in half so right sides meet

4 Sew bag opening and gussets

Bag opening
¼ (0.5)
OUTER FABRIC (RS)
¼ (0.5)
Sew running stitch using hand sewing thread (see p55 for embroidery instructions)
Gusset

5 Attach straps

<23>

18 (46)
Strap length 19¾ (50)
5½ (14)
1⁵⁄₈ (4)
10½ (26)
9½ (24)
8¾ (22)

1⁵⁄₈ (4)
OUTER FABRIC (RS)
Stitch down using hand sewing thread

11 (28)
Strap length 11½ (29)
<25>
4 (10)
1⁵⁄₈ (4)
6³⁄₈ (16)
5½ (14)
5½ (14)

14¼ (36)
Strap length 17¾ (45)
4¾ (12)
1⁵⁄₈ (4)
8¼ (21)
7 (18)
7 (18)

6 Create base board and insert

⁵⁄₈ (1.5)
⁵⁄₈ (1.5)
Poly fiber cut to same side as base
(WS)
Poly fiber
Seam allowance
Fold excess seam allowance over and secure with double sided tape
Base board fabric with extra ³⁄₈ in (1.5cm) seam allowance

26. ~ 29. Purse and Shoulder Bag with Spring Clasp

Photo: pages 20–21

● MATERIALS FOR 23

Print fabric (for outer fabric) 6 x 16 in (15 x 40cm)
Linen (for lining) 6 x 18 in (15 x 45cm)
Spring clasp (with round-headed pins) 3/8 in wide x 4 in (1cm wide x 10cm long)
Swivel latch 3/8 in wide x 1 1/8 in long (1cm wide x 3cm long) x 1
Tape for strap 5/8 in wide x 30 in (1.5cm wide x 75cm)
Hand sewing thread such as Schappe Spun brand, brown
Round nose pliers with side cutter

● MATERIALS FOR 27

Print fabric (for outer fabric) 8 x 16 in (20 x 40cm)
Linen (for lining) 8 x 42 in (20 x 45cm)
Spring clasp (with round-headed pins) 3/8 in wide x 4 3/4 in long (1cm wide x 12cm long)
Swivel latch 3/8 in wide x 1 1/8 in long x 1 (1cm wide x 3cm long x 1)
Tape for strap 5/8 in wide x 34 in (1.5cm wide x 85cm)
Hand sewing thread such as Schappe Spun brand, brown
Round nose pliers with side cutter

● MATERIALS FOR 28

Print fabric (for outer fabric) 6 x 10 in (15 x 25cm)
Linen (for lining) 6 x 12 in (15 x 30cm)
Spring clasp 3/8 in wide x 4 in long (1cm wide x 10cm long)
Hand sewing thread such as Schappe Spun brand, brown
Round nose pliers with side cutter

● MATERIALS FOR 29

Print fabric (for outer fabric) 8 x 12 in (20 x 30cm)
Linen (for lining) 8 x 14 in (20 x 35cm)
Spring clasp 3/8 in wide x 4 in long (1cm wide x 10cm long)
Hand sewing thread such as Schappe Spun brand, brown
Round nose pliers with side cutter

※ Measurements given in inches and centimeters
※○ Add figure in circle as seam allowance when drafting pattern
　　(①cm = 3/8 in; ③cm = 1 1/8 in)

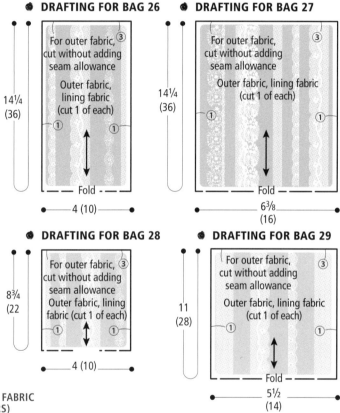

● **DRAFTING FOR BAG 26**
For outer fabric, cut without adding seam allowance
Outer fabric, lining fabric (cut 1 of each)
14 1/4 (36)
4 (10)
Fold

● **DRAFTING FOR BAG 27**
For outer fabric, cut without adding seam allowance
Outer fabric, lining fabric (cut 1 of each)
14 1/4 (36)
6 3/8 (16)
Fold

● **DRAFTING FOR BAG 28**
For outer fabric, cut without adding seam allowance
Outer fabric, lining fabric (cut 1 of each)
8 3/4 (22)
4 (10)

● **DRAFTING FOR BAG 29**
For outer fabric, cut without adding seam allowance
Outer fabric, lining fabric (cut 1 of each)
11 (28)
5 1/2 (14)
Fold

● INSTRUCTIONS FOR 26, 28

1 Match outer and lining fabrics and sew together

2 Sew bag opening

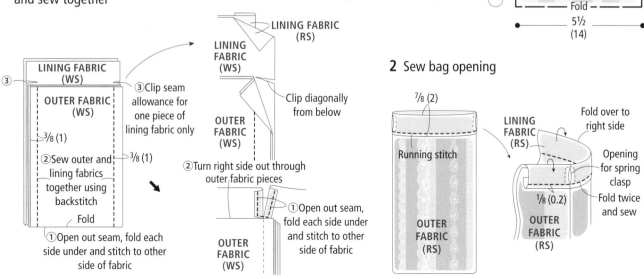

LINING FABRIC (WS)
③ OUTER FABRIC (WS)
③ Clip seam allowance for one piece of lining fabric only
3/8 (1)
② Sew outer and lining fabrics together using backstitch
3/8 (1)
Fold
① Open out seam, fold each side under and stitch to other side of fabric

LINING FABRIC (RS)
LINING FABRIC (WS)
Clip diagonally from below
OUTER FABRIC (WS)
② Turn right side out through outer fabric pieces
① Open out seam, fold each side under and stitch to other side of fabric
OUTER FABRIC (WS)

7/8 (2)
Running stitch
OUTER FABRIC (RS)
LINING FABRIC (RS)
Fold over to right side
Opening for spring clasp
1/8 (0.2)
Fold twice and sew
OUTER FABRIC (RS)

3 Insert spring clasp

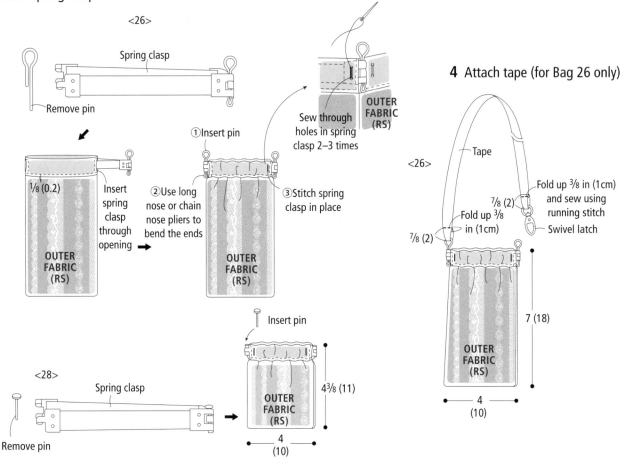

<26>

Spring clasp

Remove pin

Insert spring clasp through opening

1/8 (0.2)

① Insert pin

② Use long nose or chain nose pliers to bend the ends

③ Stitch spring clasp in place

Sew through holes in spring clasp 2–3 times

OUTER FABRIC (RS)

OUTER FABRIC (RS)

OUTER FABRIC (RS)

<28>

Spring clasp

Remove pin

Insert pin

OUTER FABRIC (RS)

4 3/8 (11)

4 (10)

4 Attach tape (for Bag 26 only)

<26>

Tape

Fold up 3/8 in (1cm) and sew using running stitch

7/8 (2)

Swivel latch

Fold up 3/8 in (1cm)

7/8 (2)

7 (18)

OUTER FABRIC (RS)

4 (10)

● INSTRUCTIONS FOR 27, 29

1 Match outer and lining sections and sew together

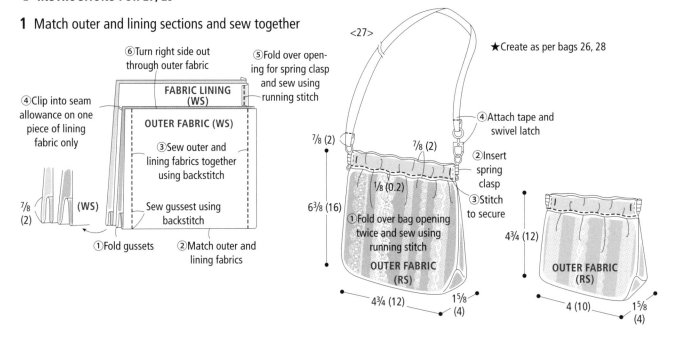

⑥ Turn right side out through outer fabric

⑤ Fold over opening for spring clasp and sew using running stitch

④ Clip into seam allowance on one piece of lining fabric only

FABRIC LINING (WS)

OUTER FABRIC (WS)

③ Sew outer and lining fabrics together using backstitch

Sew gusset using backstitch

7/8 (2)

(WS)

① Fold gussets

② Match outer and lining fabrics

2 Sew bag opening and attach spring clasp and tape

<27>

★Create as per bags 26, 28

④ Attach tape and swivel latch

② Insert spring clasp

③ Stitch to secure

7/8 (2)

7/8 (2)

1/8 (0.2)

6 3/8 (16)

① Fold over bag opening twice and sew using running stitch

OUTER FABRIC (RS)

4 3/4 (12)

1 5/8 (4)

4 3/4 (12)

OUTER FABRIC (RS)

4 (10)

1 5/8 (4)

39. Bag with Frame

Photo: page 24

● MATERIALS

Double layer gauze (for outer fabric) 20 x 8 in (50 x 20cm)

Print fabric (for lining and decorative fabric) 24 x 8 in
  (60 x 20cm)

Quilt wadding (thin) 20 x 8 in (50 x 20cm)

Lace ³⁄₈ in wide x 16 in (1cm wide x 40cm)

Frame (with round holes for straps and paper braid)
  4³⁄₄ x 2 in (12 x 5cm) x 1

Glass beads 12mm diameter x 2

Hand sewing thread such as MOCO brand, pale blue

Hand sewing thread such as Schappe Spun brand,
  pale blue

Crochet hook size 7/0

Glue

Screwdriver

Pliers

● USE FULL-SIZE PATTERN PIECE SIDE B

※ Measurements given in inches and centimeters

※○ Add figure in circle as seam allowance when
  drafting pattern
  (①cm = ³⁄₈ in)

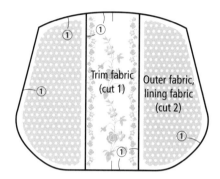

Trim fabric (cut 1)

Outer fabric, lining fabric (cut 2)

● INSTRUCTIONS

1 Create trim

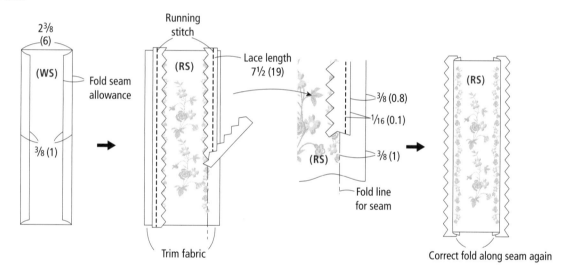

2³⁄₈ (6)

(WS)

Fold seam allowance

³⁄₈ (1)

Running stitch

(RS)

Trim fabric

Lace length 7¹⁄₂ (19)

(RS)

³⁄₈ (0.8)

¹⁄₁₆ (0.1)

³⁄₈ (1)

Fold line for seam

(RS)

Correct fold along seam again

2 Attach trim to outer fabric

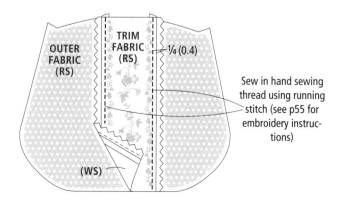

OUTER FABRIC (RS)

TRIM FABRIC (RS)

¹⁄₄ (0.4)

Sew in hand sewing thread using running stitch (see p55 for embroidery instructions)

(WS)

3 Sew outer fabric, lining fabric and quilt wadding together

5 Create strap and attach to bag

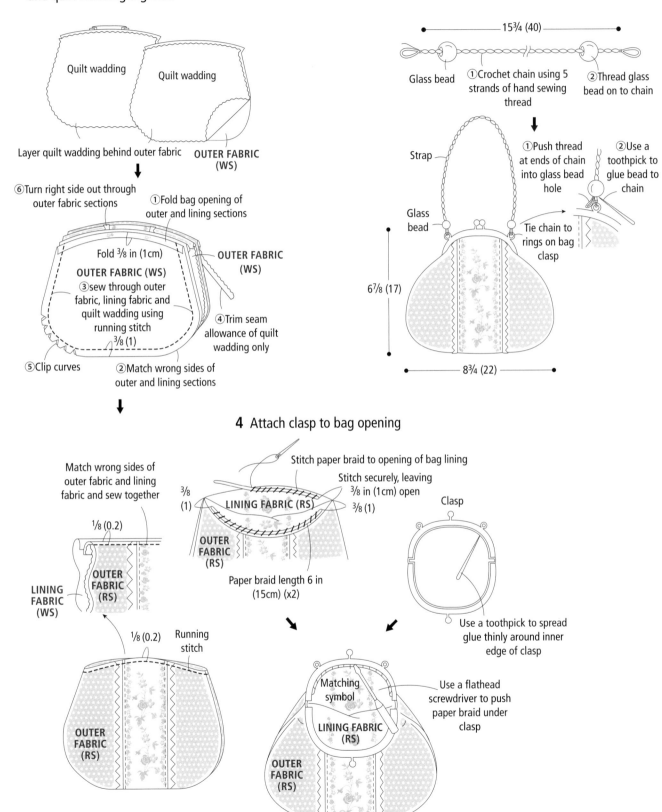

Quilt wadding

Quilt wadding

Layer quilt wadding behind outer fabric

OUTER FABRIC (WS)

⑥Turn right side out through outer fabric sections

①Fold bag opening of outer and lining sections

Fold ³/₈ in (1cm)

OUTER FABRIC (WS)

OUTER FABRIC (WS)

③sew through outer fabric, lining fabric and quilt wadding using running stitch ³/₈ (1)

④Trim seam allowance of quilt wadding only

⑤Clip curves

②Match wrong sides of outer and lining sections

15¾ (40)

Glass bead

①Crochet chain using 5 strands of hand sewing thread

②Thread glass bead on to chain

Strap

①Push thread at ends of chain into glass bead hole

②Use a toothpick to glue bead to chain

Glass bead

6⅞ (17)

Tie chain to rings on bag clasp

8¾ (22)

4 Attach clasp to bag opening

Match wrong sides of outer fabric and lining fabric and sew together

Stitch paper braid to opening of bag lining

Stitch securely, leaving ³/₈ in (1cm) open

Clasp

⅛ (0.2)

³/₈ (1)

LINING FABRIC (RS)

³/₈ (1)

OUTER FABRIC (RS)

OUTER FABRIC (RS)

LINING FABRIC (WS)

OUTER FABRIC (RS)

Paper braid length 6 in (15cm) (x2)

Use a toothpick to spread glue thinly around inner edge of clasp

⅛ (0.2)

Running stitch

OUTER FABRIC (RS)

Matching symbol

Use a flathead screwdriver to push paper braid under clasp

LINING FABRIC (RS)

OUTER FABRIC (RS)

40. Bag with Frame

Photo: page 25

MATERIALS

- Double layer gauze (for outer fabric, lining, base board fabric) 24 x 18 in (60 x 45cm)
- Linen gingham (for base fabric) 10 x 8 in (25 x 20cm)
- Print fabric (for appliqué) 4 x 4 in (10 x 10cm)
- Quilt wadding (thin) 10 x 16 in (25 x 40cm)
- Poly fiber (for base board) 4 x 6 in (10 x 15 cm)
- Lace 4 x 6 in (10 x 15cm)
- Frame (with round holes for straps and paper braid) 4¾ x 2 in (12 x 5cm) x 1
- Glass beads 12mm diameter x 2
- Hand sewing thread such as MOCO brand, green
- Hand sewing thread such as Schappe Spun brand, light green

- Crochet hook size 7/0
- Glue
- Screwdriver
- Pliers

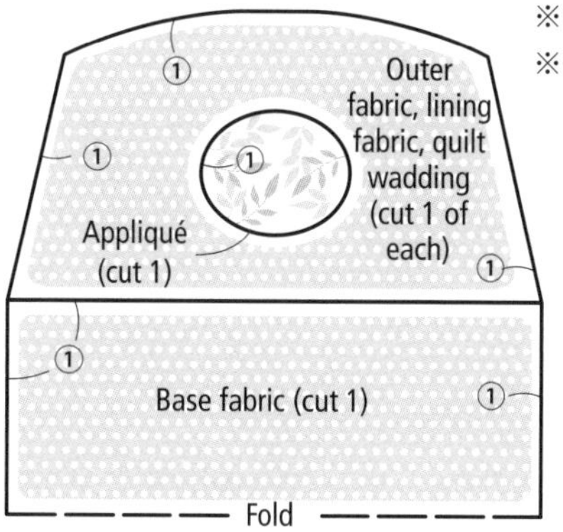

①
①
①
Outer fabric, lining fabric, quilt wadding (cut 1 of each)
Appliqué (cut 1)
①
①
Base fabric (cut 1)
①
Fold

USE FULL-SIZE PATTERN PIECE SIDE B

※ Measurements given in inches and centimeters

※○ Add figure in circle as seam allowance when drafting pattern

(①cm = ⅜ in; ⑮cm = ⅝ in)

DRAFTING

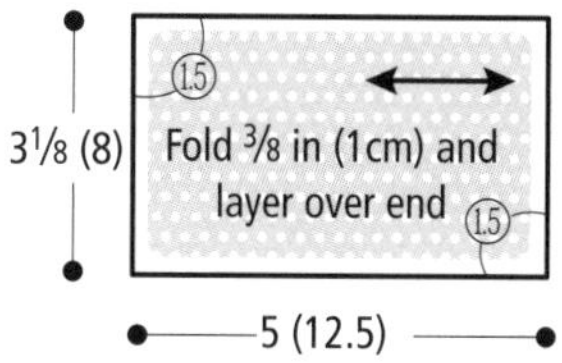

⑮
Fold ⅜ in (1cm) and layer over end
⑮
3⅛ (8)
5 (12.5)

INSTRUCTIONS

1 Create appliqué and attach to outer fabric

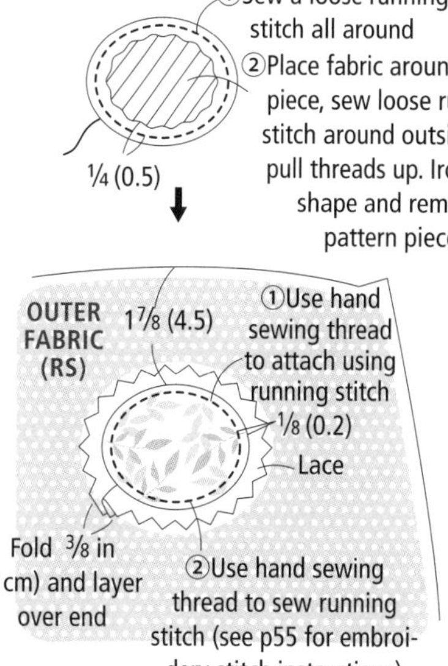

①Sew a loose running stitch all around
②Place fabric around pattern piece, sew loose running stitch around outside and pull threads up. Iron into shape and remove pattern piece
¼ (0.5)
OUTER FABRIC (RS)
1⅞ (4.5)
①Use hand sewing thread to attach using running stitch
⅛ (0.2)
Lace
Fold ⅜ in (1cm) and layer over end
②Use hand sewing thread to sew running stitch (see p55 for embroidery stitch instructions)

2 Attach base fabric to outer fabric, layer quilt wadding underneath

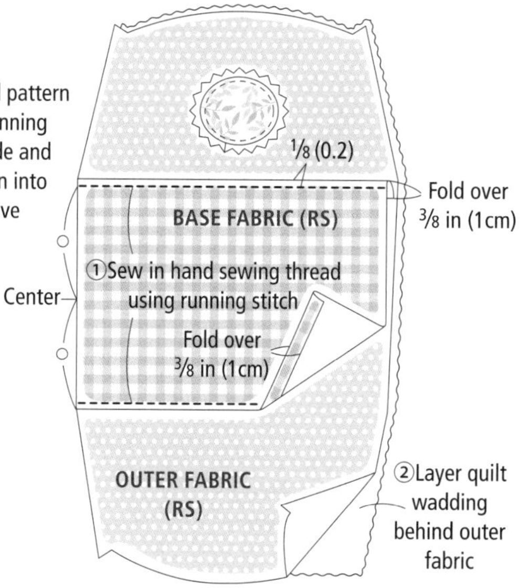

⅛ (0.2)
Fold over ⅜ in (1cm)
BASE FABRIC (RS)
Center
①Sew in hand sewing thread using running stitch
Fold over ⅜ in (1cm)
OUTER FABRIC (RS)
②Layer quilt wadding behind outer fabric

3 Sew together outer fabric and lining fabric

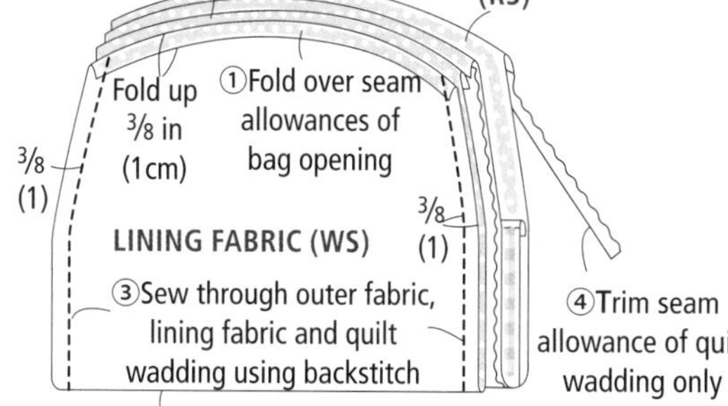

⑤Turn bag right side out through lining
OUTER FABRIC (RS)
Fold up ⅜ in (1cm)
①Fold over seam allowances of bag opening
⅜ (1)
⅜ (1)
LINING FABRIC (WS)
③Sew through outer fabric, lining fabric and quilt wadding using backstitch
④Trim seam allowance of quilt wadding only
②Fold outer fabric and lining fabric in half and place together

4 Sew bag and opening gussets

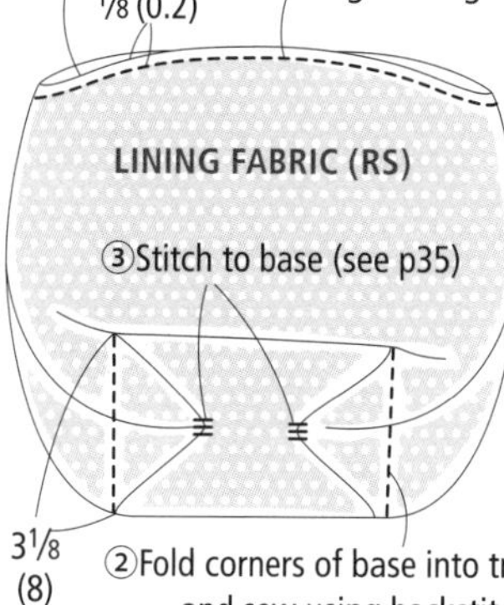

④Turn right side out
①Match wrong sides of outer fabric and lining and sew using running stitch
⅛ (0.2)
LINING FABRIC (RS)
③Stitch to base (see p35)
3⅛ (8)
②Fold corners of base into triangles and sew using backstitch

5 Attach clasp and strap

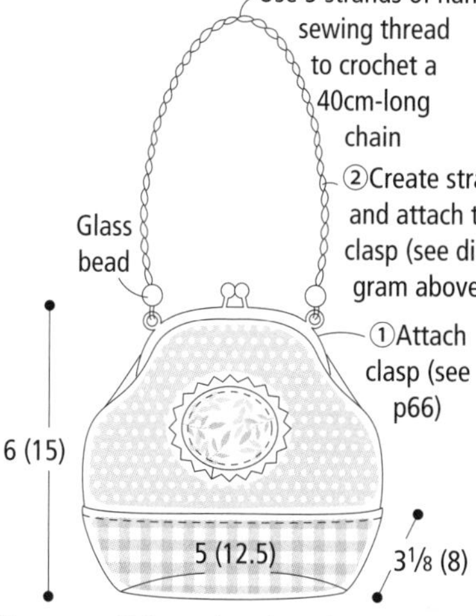

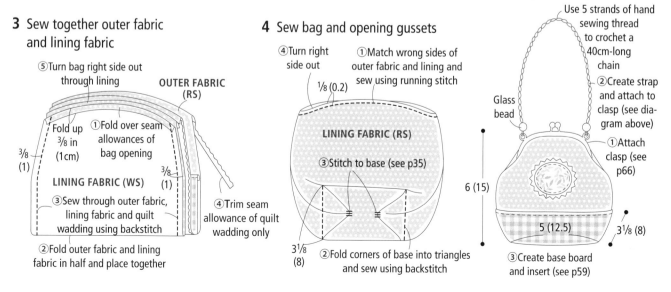

Use 5 strands of hand sewing thread to crochet a 40cm-long chain
②Create strap and attach to clasp (see diagram above)
Glass bead
①Attach clasp (see p66)
6 (15)
5 (12.5)
3⅛ (8)
③Create base board and insert (see p59)

41, 42. Small Bag

Photo: pages 26–27

● MATERIALS FOR 41

Linen (for outer fabric, lining) 38 x 10 in (95 x 25cm)
Lace 2¼ in wide x 10 in (5.5cm wide x 25cm), 1⅛ in
  wide x 18 in (3cm wide x 45cm)
Glass bead 12mm diameter x 1
Hand sewing thread such as MOCO brand, neutral
Hand sewing thread such as Schappe Spun brand,
  white
Crochet hook size 3/0

● MATERIALS FOR 42

Cotton voile (for outer fabric) 20 x 10 in (50 x 25cm)
Linen (for lining) 20 x 10 in (50 x 25cm)
Tassel 3½ in (9cm) long x 1
Glass beads 12mm diameter x 5, 8mm x 6, 6mm x 12
Hand sewing thread such as MOCO brand, neutral
Hand sewing thread (fine), white
Crochet hook size 3/0

● USE FULL-SIZE PATTERN PIECE SIDE A

※ Measurements given in inches and centimeters
※○ Add figure in circle as seam allowance when
  drafting pattern
  (①cm = ⅜ in)

● INSTRUCTIONS

1 Attach lace to one side of
   outer fabric (only for Bag 41)

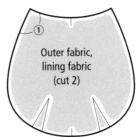

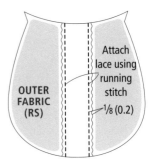

2 Sew darts in outer fabric and lining fabric

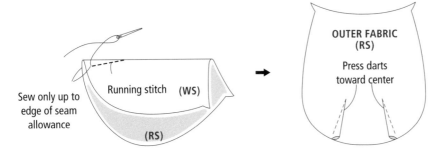

3 Fold opening of outer fabric and lining fabric

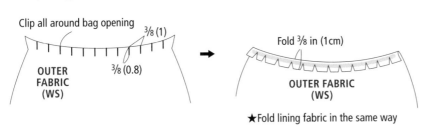

4 Sew outer fabric and
   lining fabric together

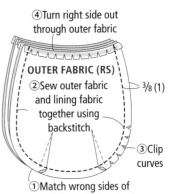

68

5 Create strap

<41> Fold lace in half and sew

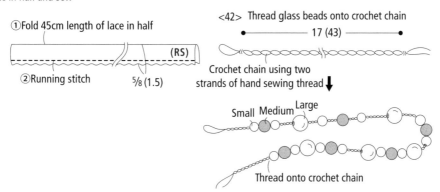

① Fold 45cm length of lace in half

② Running stitch   5/8 (1.5)   (RS)

<42> Thread glass beads onto crochet chain

17 (43)

Crochet chain using two
strands of hand sewing thread ⬇

Small Medium Large

Thread onto crochet chain

6 Sew bag opening

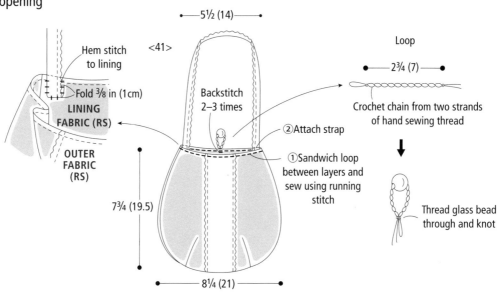

Hem stitch
to lining

Fold 3/8 in (1cm)

LINING
FABRIC (RS)

OUTER
FABRIC
(RS)

<41>

5½ (14)

Backstitch
2–3 times

② Attach strap

① Sandwich loop
between layers and
sew using running
stitch

7¾ (19.5)

8¼ (21)

Loop

2¾ (7)

Crochet chain from two strands
of hand sewing thread

⬇

Thread glass bead
through and knot

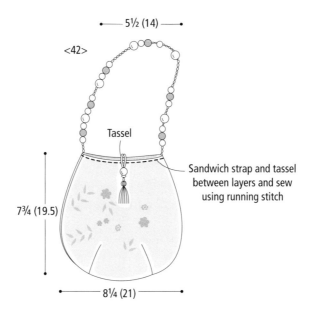

5½ (14)

<42>

Tassel

Sandwich strap and tassel
between layers and sew
using running stitch

7¾ (19.5)

8¼ (21)

69

17. 18. Tote Bag with Gusset

Photo: page 14

MATERIALS FOR 17

Striped fabric (for bag) 14 x 30 in (35 x 75cm)
Fusible belt interfacing 1⅝ in wide x 22 in (4cm wide x 55cm)
Leather strip (for handles) ⅜ in wide x 13 in long (1cm wide x 33cm long)
Hand sewing thread such as MOCO brand, light purple
Hand sewing thread such as Schappe Spun brand, beige

MATERIALS FOR 18

Gingham (for bag) 20 x 36 in (50 x 90cm)
Striped fabric (for pocket) 6 x 6 in (15 x 15cm)
Fusible belt interfacing 1⅝ in wide x 36 in (4cm wide x 90cm)
Leather strip (for handles) ¾ in wide x 16 in (1.7cm wide x 40cm)
Hand sewing thread such as MOCO brand, light purple
Hand sewing thread such as Schappe Spun brand, beige

※ Measurements given in inches and centimeters

※○ Add figure in circle as seam allowance when drafting pattern
(⑮cm = ⅝ in; ③cm = 1⅛ in; ⑥cm = 2⅜ in)

● DRAFTING FOR BAG 18

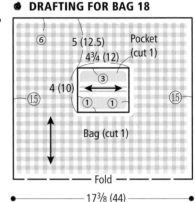

● DRAFTING FOR BAG 17

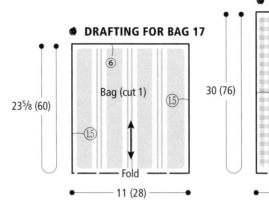

● DRAFTING FOR BAG 18

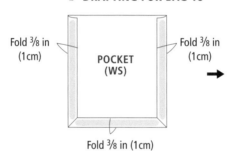

※See p35 for instructions and finished measurements for bags 17, 18

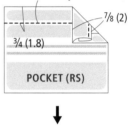

Use hand sewing thread to sew using running stitch (see p55 for embroidery instructions)

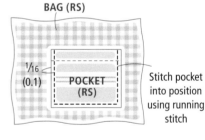

Stitch pocket into position using running stitch

● FULL-SIZE EMBROIDERY DIAGRAM FOR BAG 60

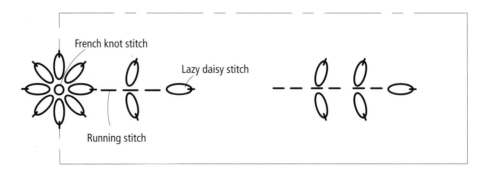

French knot stitch

Lazy daisy stitch

Running stitch

43.44. Bag with Lace-trim Zipper (S, L)

Photo: pages 28–29

● MATERIALS FOR 43

Linen (for outer fabric, lining, outer fabric for base, lining for base, pocket, base board fabric) 42 x 14 in (105 x 35cm)

Check fabric (for self-cover buttons) 4 x 2 in (10 x 5cm)

Fusible interfacing (thin) 24 x 8 in (60 x 20cm)

Poly fiber (for base board) 6 x 4 in (15 x 10cm)

Leather strip (for handle) $3/8$ in wide x 13 in (1cm wide x 33cm)

Lace-trim zipper (double-ended) 14 in (35cm) x 1

Buttons $3/4$ in (1.8cm) diameter, $5/8$ in (1.5cm) diameter, $1/2$ in (1.2cm) diameter x 1 each

Hand sewing thread such as MOCO brand, red

Hand sewing thread such as Schappe Spun brand, red, beige

● MATERIALS FOR 44

Linen (for outer fabric, lining, outer fabric for base, lining for base, base board fabric) 44 x 20 in (110 x 50cm)

Fusible interfacing (thin) 32 x 14 in (80 x 35cm)

Poly fiber (for base board) 10 x 6 in (25 x 15cm)

Leather strip (for handle) $7/8$ in wide x 18 in (2cm wide x 44cm)

Lace-trim zipper (double-ended) 14 in (35cm) x 1

Flower motif (S) x 2, (M) x 3

Hand sewing thread such as MOCO brand, dark brown, ocher

Hand sewing thread such as Schappe Spun brand, brown, beige

※ Measurements given in inches and centimeters

※○ Add figure in circle as seam allowance when drafting pattern (①cm = $3/8$ in; ⑮ cm = $5/8$ in)

● FOR BAG 44, USE FULL-SIZE PATTERN PIECE SIDE B

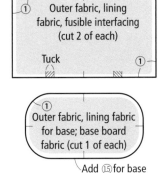

Outer fabric, lining fabric, fusible interfacing (cut 2 of each)

Tuck

Outer fabric, lining fabric for base; base board fabric (cut 1 of each)

Add ⑮ for base board fabric

● FOR BAG 43, USE FULL-SIZE PATTERN PIECE SIDE B

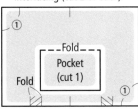

Outer fabric, lining fabric, fusible interfacing (cut 2 of each)

Fold

Pocket (cut 1)

Fold

Add ⑮ for base board fabric

Outer fabric, lining fabric for base; base board fabric (cut 1 of each)

● INSTRUCTIONS FOR BAG 44

1 Attach fusible interfacing to outer fabric and outer base fabric (use dry iron on medium heat)

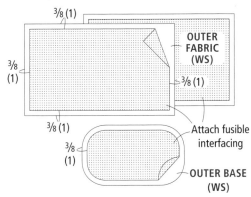

$3/8$ (1)

$3/8$ (1)

$3/8$ (1)

$3/8$ (1)

$3/8$ (1)

OUTER FABRIC (WS)

Attach fusible interfacing

OUTER BASE (WS)

2 Complete embroidery and attach flowers

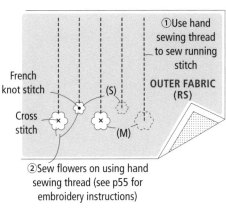

①Use hand sewing thread to sew running stitch

OUTER FABRIC (RS)

French knot stitch

Cross stitch

(S)

(M)

②Sew flowers on using hand sewing thread (see p55 for embroidery instructions)

3 Fold tucks and stitch in place

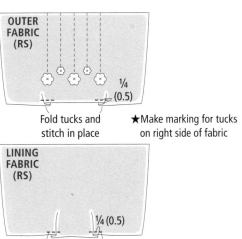

OUTER FABRIC (RS)

$1/4$ (0.5)

Fold tucks and stitch in place

★Make marking for tucks on right side of fabric

LINING FABRIC (RS)

$1/4$ (0.5)

Fold tucks and stitch in place

4 Sew outer fabric and sew to outer base fabric

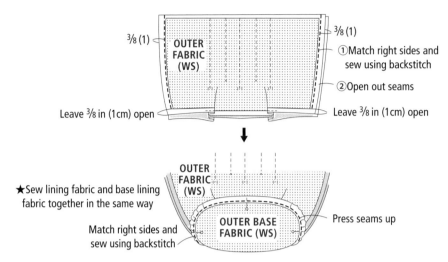

3/8 (1)

3/8 (1)

OUTER FABRIC (WS)

①Match right sides and sew using backstitch

②Open out seams

Leave 3/8 in (1cm) open

Leave 3/8 in (1cm) open

★Sew lining fabric and base lining fabric together in the same way

OUTER FABRIC (WS)

Match right sides and sew using backstitch

OUTER BASE FABRIC (WS)

Press seams up

5 Match wrong sides of outer fabric and lining and sew bag opening

LINING (RS)

Fold 3/8 in (1cm)

LINING (WS)

①Fold over seam allowance of bag opening

OUTER FABRIC (RS)

②Match wrong sides of outer fabric and lining fabric

LINING (WS)

OUTER FABRIC (RS)

1/8 (0.2)

OUTER FABRIC (RS)

Running stitch

6 Attach lace trimmed zipper

①Backstitch

5/8 (1.5)

②Hem stitch

OUTER FABRIC (RS)

Fold end

Attach lace trimmed zipper using backstitch

5/8 (1.5)

5/8 (1.5)

OUTER FABRIC (RS)

7 Attach strap

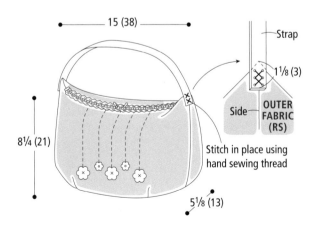

15 (38)

Strap

1 1/8 (3)

Side

OUTER FABRIC (RS)

8 1/4 (21)

Stitch in place using hand sewing thread

5 1/8 (13)

8 Create base board and insert

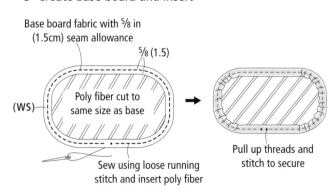

Base board fabric with 5/8 in (1.5cm) seam allowance

5/8 (1.5)

Poly fiber cut to same size as base

(WS)

Sew using loose running stitch and insert poly fiber

Pull up threads and stitch to secure

● INSTRUCTIONS FOR BAG 43

1 Attach fusible interfacing to outer fabric and outer base fabric (use dry iron on medium heat)

※See p71 for instructions

2 Cut lace trimmed zipper

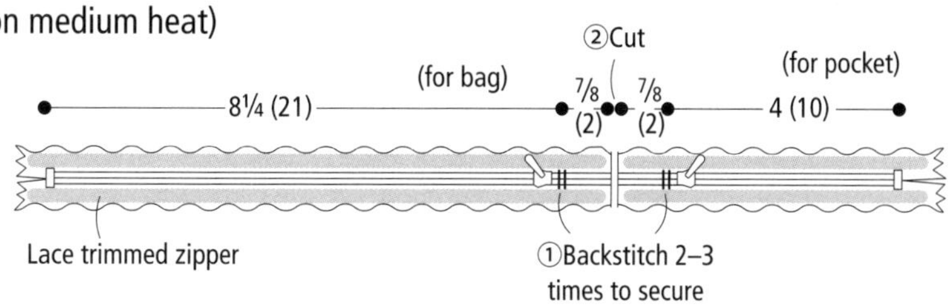

②Cut

8¼ (21) (for bag) ⅞ (2) ⅞ (2) 4 (10) (for pocket)

Lace trimmed zipper

①Backstitch 2–3 times to secure

9 (23)

★Create as for Bag 44

4 Finish bag

③Match wrong sides of outer fabric and lining fabric and sew bag opening, attach lace trimmed zipper

⅜ (1)

1⅛ (3)

④Sew strap to bag using hand sewing thread

6⅜ (16)

②Sew both edges of outer fabric and lining fabric and attach each to base fabric

3½ (9)

①Create tucks

⑤Create base board and insert (see p72)

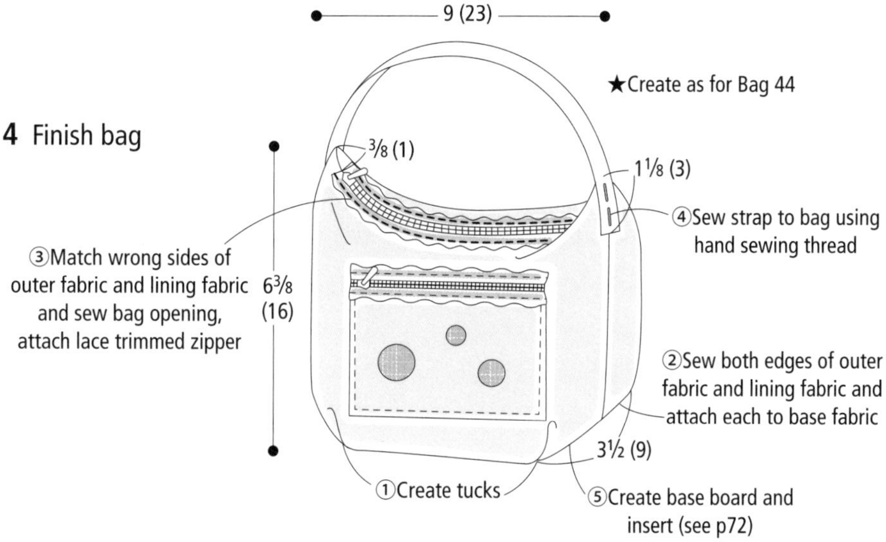

3 Create pocket and attach to outer fabric

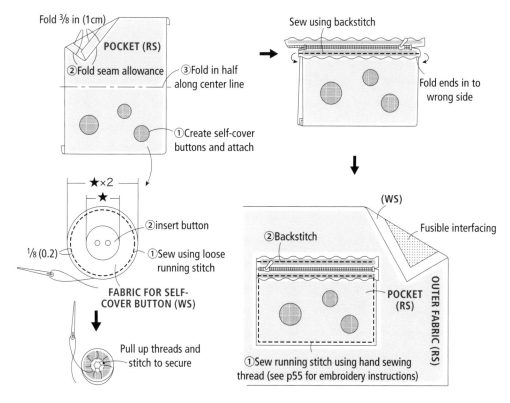

Fold ⅜ in (1cm)

POCKET (RS)

②Fold seam allowance

③Fold in half along center line

①Create self-cover buttons and attach

Sew using backstitch

Fold ends in to wrong side

★×2

★

⅛ (0.2)

②insert button

①Sew using loose running stitch

FABRIC FOR SELF-COVER BUTTON (WS)

Pull up threads and stitch to secure

(WS)

Fusible interfacing

②Backstitch

POCKET (RS)

OUTER FABRIC (RS)

①Sew running stitch using hand sewing thread (see p55 for embroidery instructions)

45. ~ 58. Vase-shaped Bag

Photo: pages 30–31

MATERIALS FOR 45

Striped fabric (for outer fabric, lining, outer fabric for base, lining for base, handles, loops) 22 x 26 in (55 x 65cm)
Fusible quilt wadding (medium thickness) 18 x 14 in (45 x 35cm)
Fusible belt interfacing 1 1/8 in wide x 14 in (3cm wide x 35cm)
Acrylic bead 15mm diameter (with large hole) x 1
Sequins 1/4 in (0.6cm), small round beads as desired
Hand sewing thread such as Schappe Spun brand, pale green, pale blue, pink

MATERIALS FOR 46

Yarn-dyed fabric (for outer fabric, lining, outer fabric for base, lining for base, handles, loops) 22 x 26 in (55 x 65cm)
Printed fabric (for appliqué) 8 x 8 in (20 x 20cm)
Fusible quilt wadding (medium thickness) 18 x 14 (45 x 35cm)
Fusible belt interfacing 1 1/8 in wide x 14 in (3cm wide x 35cm)
Acrylic bead 15mm diameter (with large hole) x 1
Heat-bondable double-sided sheet 8 x 8 in (20 x 20cm)
Hand sewing thread such as Schappe Spun brand, pink, dark pink

Bag No	Outer fabric lining fabric 22x26 in (55×65cm)	Decorations
47	cut dobby	running stitch, French knot stitch (hand sewing thread in gradated pale blues), sequins 1/4 in (0.6cm)
48	check	flower motifs 1/2 in (1.4cm), small round beads
49	cut dobby	drop beads (4mm)
50	stripe	flower motifs 1/2 in, 1 1/4 in (1.4cm, 3.3cm), small round beads
51	stripe	self-cover buttons 7/8 in (2cm) diameter, sequins 1/4 in (0.6cm) small round beads, large round beads
52	pre-dyed	appliqué, sequins 1/2 in (0.6cm)
53	print	small round beads
54	cut dobby	lazy daisy stitch (hand sewing thread in gradated orange shades), sequins 1/4 x 1/4 in (0.6 × 0.6cm), large round beads
55	plain	appliqué, pearl beads (4mm)
56	cut dobby	outline stitch (hand sewing threads in gradated orange shades), drop beads (4mm)
57	check	flower motifs 1/2 in (1.4cm), beads (like those used for an abacus, 4mm)
58	stripe	sequins (0.6cm)

USE FULL-SIZE PATTERN PIECE SIDE B

※ Measurements given in inches and centimeters
※○ Add figure in circle as seam allowance when drafting pattern (①cm = 3/8 in; ⑮cm = 5/8 in)

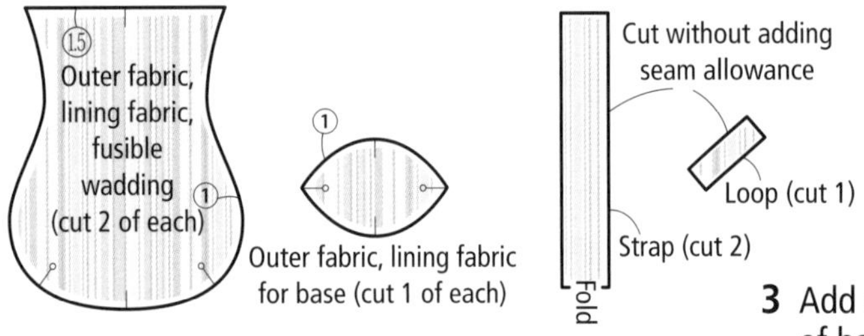
⑮
Outer fabric, lining fabric, fusible wadding (cut 2 of each)
①
①
Outer fabric, lining fabric for base (cut 1 of each)
Cut without adding seam allowance
Loop (cut 1)
Strap (cut 2)
Fold

INSTRUCTIONS

1 Cut out fusible wadding

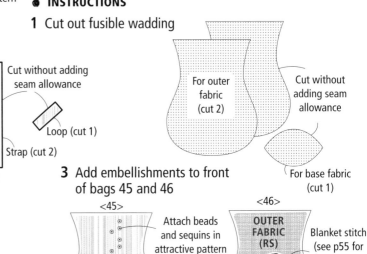

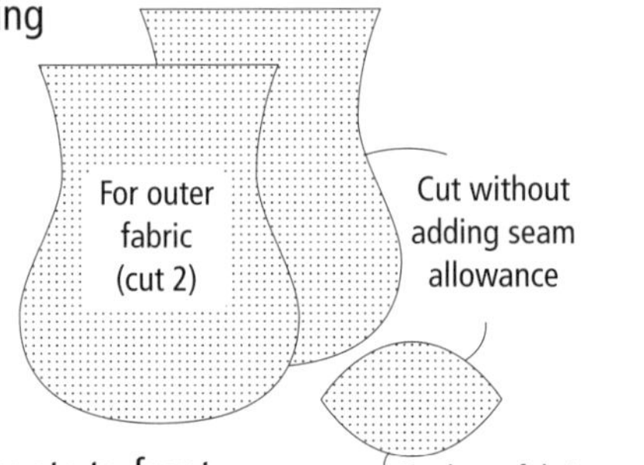
For outer fabric (cut 2)
Cut without adding seam allowance
For base fabric (cut 1)

2 Attach fusible wadding to outer fabric and outer base fabric (use dry iron on medium heat)

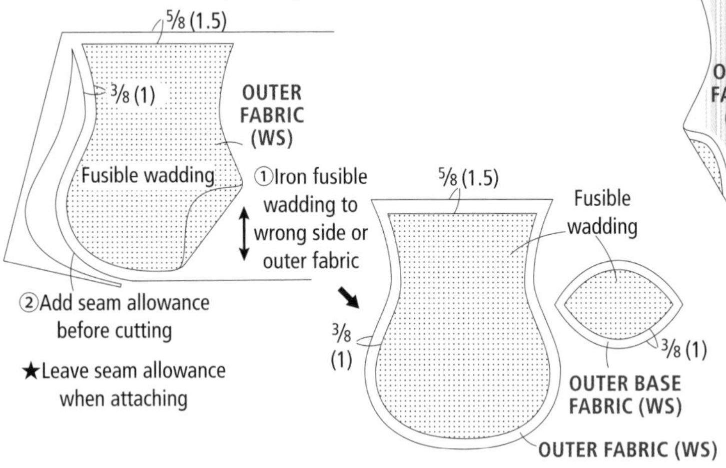
5/8 (1.5)
3/8 (1)
OUTER FABRIC (WS)
Fusible wadding
①Iron fusible wadding to wrong side or outer fabric
②Add seam allowance before cutting
★Leave seam allowance when attaching
5/8 (1.5)
Fusible wadding
3/8 (1)
3/8 (1)
OUTER BASE FABRIC (WS)
OUTER FABRIC (WS)

3 Add embellishments to front of bags 45 and 46

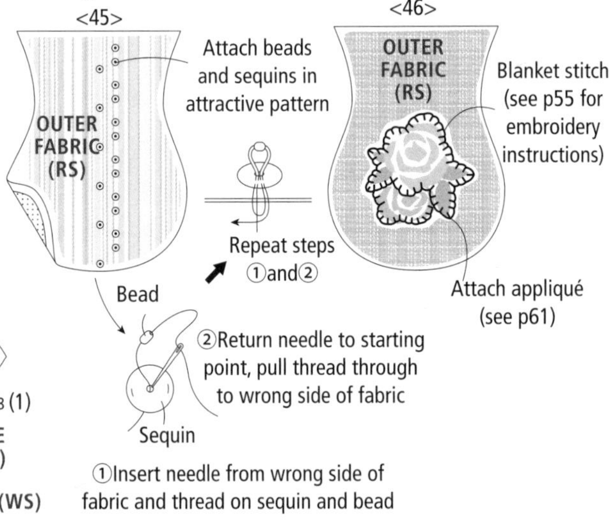
<45>
Attach beads and sequins in attractive pattern
OUTER FABRIC (RS)
Repeat steps ①and②
Bead
②Return needle to starting point, pull thread through to wrong side of fabric
Sequin
①Insert needle from wrong side of fabric and thread on sequin and bead
<46>
OUTER FABRIC (RS)
Blanket stitch (see p55 for embroidery instructions)
Attach appliqué (see p61)

4 Attach adhesive belt interfacing to opening of lining (use dry iron on medium heat)

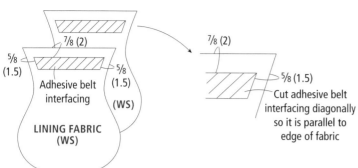

⁷⁄₈ (2)

⁵⁄₈ (1.5)

⁵⁄₈ (1.5)

Adhesive belt interfacing

(WS)

LINING FABRIC (WS)

⁷⁄₈ (2)

⁵⁄₈ (1.5)

Cut adhesive belt interfacing diagonally so it is parallel to edge of fabric

5 Sew outer fabric and lining fabric together

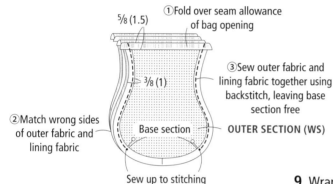

⁵⁄₈ (1.5)

① Fold over seam allowance of bag opening

³⁄₈ (1)

③ Sew outer fabric and lining fabric together using backstitch, leaving base section free

OUTER SECTION (WS)

② Match wrong sides of outer fabric and lining fabric

Base section

Sew up to stitching endpoint

6 Sew outer base fabric and base lining fabric together

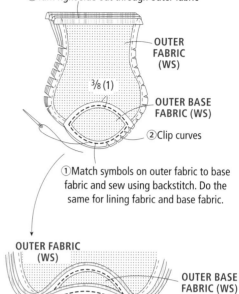

③ Turn right side out through outer fabric

OUTER FABRIC (WS)

³⁄₈ (1)

OUTER BASE FABRIC (WS)

② Clip curves

① Match symbols on outer fabric to base fabric and sew using backstitch. Do the same for lining fabric and base fabric.

OUTER FABRIC (WS)

OUTER BASE FABRIC (WS)

BASE LINING FABRIC (WS)

7 Sew straps and loop

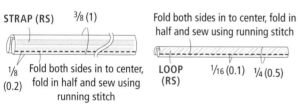

STRAP (RS)

³⁄₈ (1)

¹⁄₈ (0.2)

Fold both sides in to center, fold in half and sew using running stitch

Fold both sides in to center, fold in half and sew using running stitch

LOOP (RS)

¹⁄₁₆ (0.1)

¹⁄₄ (0.5)

8 Sandwich loop and straps in between layers of bag opening and sew

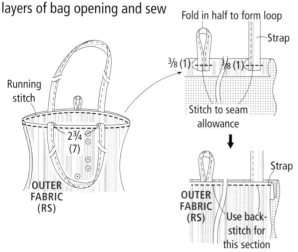

Running stitch

2³⁄₄ (7)

OUTER FABRIC (RS)

Fold in half to form loop

Strap

³⁄₈ (1)

³⁄₈ (1)

Stitch to seam allowance

Strap

OUTER FABRIC (RS)

Use backstitch for this section

9 Wrap thread around bead and attach

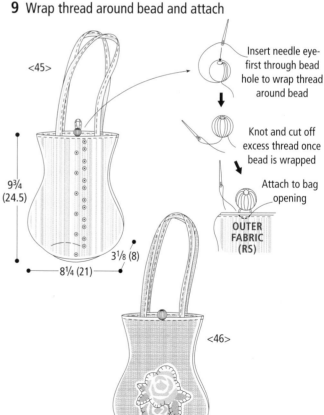

<45>

9³⁄₄ (24.5)

8¹⁄₄ (21)

3¹⁄₈ (8)

Insert needle eye-first through bead hole to wrap thread around bead

Knot and cut off excess thread once bead is wrapped

Attach to bag opening

OUTER FABRIC (RS)

<46>

59. Tucked Bag with Corsage

Photo: page 32

● MATERIALS FOR BAG

Printed fabric (for outer fabric, opening of bag)
  26 x 26 in (65 x 65cm)
Linen gingham (for lining, base board fabric)
  24 x 18 in (60 x 45cm)
Adhesive belt interfacing 1⅝ in wide x 24 in
  (4cm wide x 60cm)
Poly fiber (for base board) 16 x 4 in (40 x 10cm)
Punched leather tape (for handles) ⅝ in wide x
  44 in (1.5cm wide x 110cm)
Magnet fasteners (sew-on type) x 1 set
Hand sewing thread such as MOCO brand,
  dark pink
Hand sewing thread such as Schappe Spun brand,
  pink, red

● MATERIALS FOR CORSAGE

Printed fabric 6 x 14 in (15 x 35cm)
Lightweight fusible interfacing 6 x 14 in
  (15 x 35cm)
Button ⅞ in (2cm) diameter x 1
Brooch pin 1⅛ in (3cm) long x 1
Hand sewing thread such as Schappe Spun
  brand, pink

※ Measurements given in inches and
  centimeters
※○ Add figure in circle as seam
  allowance when drafting pattern
  (①cm = ⅜ in; ⑮ cm = ⅝ in)

● DRAFTING FOR BAG

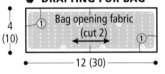

4 (10)
Bag opening fabric (cut 2)
12 (30)

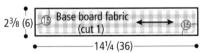

2⅜ (6)
Base board fabric (cut 1)
14¼ (36)

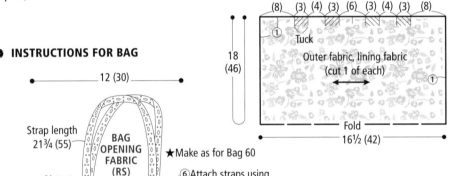

3⅛ (8) 1⅛ (3) 1⅝ (4) 1⅛ (3) 2⅜ (6) 1⅛ (3) 1⅝ (4) 1⅛ (3) 3⅛ (8)

18 (46)

Tuck
Outer fabric, lining fabric (cut 1 of each)
Fold
16½ (42)

● DRAFTING FOR CORSAGE

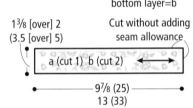

top layer=a
bottom layer=b

Cut without adding
seam allowance

1⅜ [over] 2 (3.5 [over] 5)

a (cut 1) b (cut 2)

9⅞ (25)
13 (33)

● INSTRUCTIONS FOR BAG

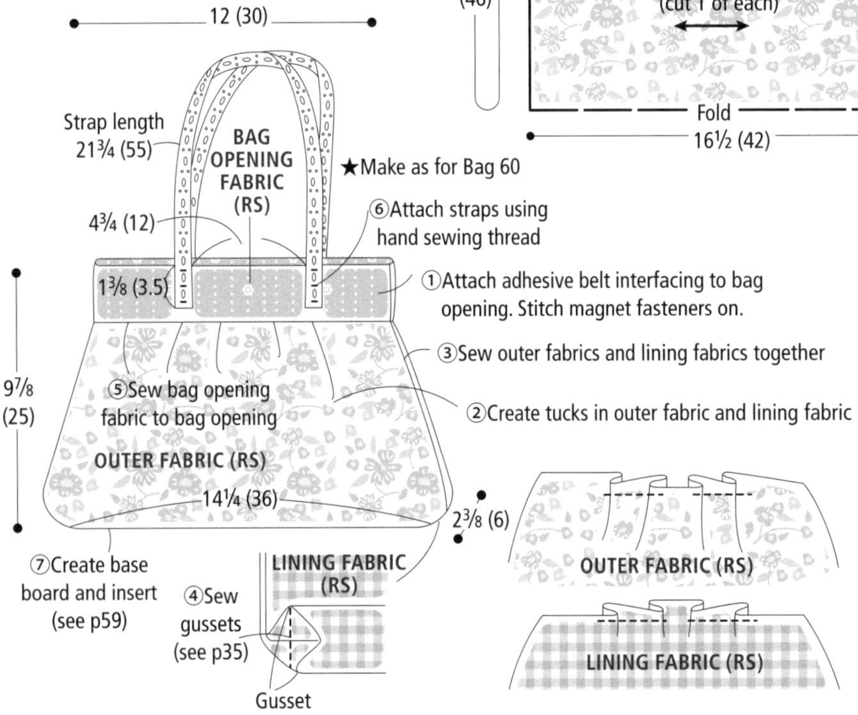

12 (30)

Strap length 21¾ (55)

BAG OPENING FABRIC (RS)

4¾ (12)

1⅜ (3.5)

9⅞ (25)

★Make as for Bag 60

⑥Attach straps using hand sewing thread

⑤Sew bag opening fabric to bag opening

OUTER FABRIC (RS)

14¼ (36)

⑦Create base board and insert (see p59)

④Sew gussets (see p35)

Gusset

LINING FABRIC (RS)

①Attach adhesive belt interfacing to bag opening. Stitch magnet fasteners on.

③Sew outer fabrics and lining fabrics together

②Create tucks in outer fabric and lining fabric

2⅜ (6)

OUTER FABRIC (RS)

LINING FABRIC (RS)

● FULL-SIZE TEMPLATE FOR CORSAGE

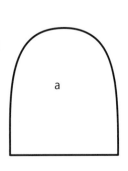

a

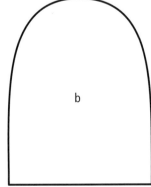

b

● INSTRUCTIONS FOR CORSAGE

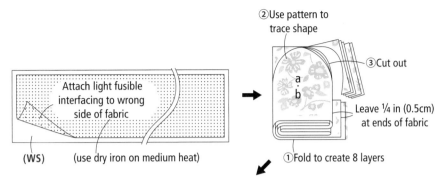

Attach light fusible interfacing to wrong side of fabric

(WS)

(use dry iron on medium heat)

② Use pattern to trace shape

③ Cut out

a
·
b

Leave ¼ in (0.5cm) at ends of fabric

① Fold to create 8 layers

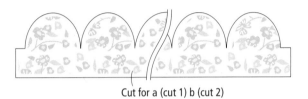

Cut for a (cut 1) b (cut 2)

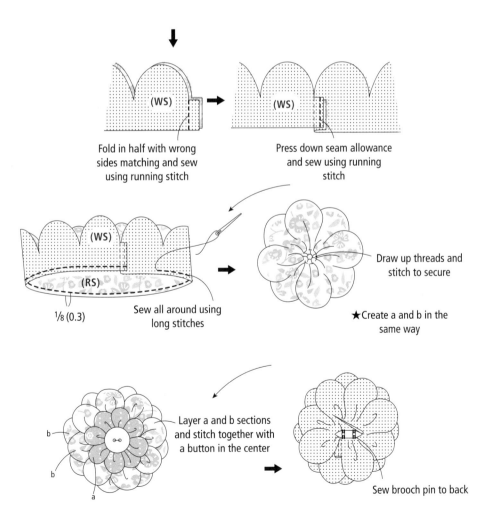

(WS)

Fold in half with wrong sides matching and sew using running stitch

(WS)

Press down seam allowance and sew using running stitch

(WS)

(RS)

⅛ (0.3)

Sew all around using long stitches

Draw up threads and stitch to secure

★ Create a and b in the same way

b

b

a

Layer a and b sections and stitch together with a button in the center

Sew brooch pin to back

77

60. Tucked Bag with Floral Embroidery

Photo: page 33

❀ MATERIALS

Linen gingham (for outer fabric) 14 x 22 in (35 x 55cm)

Linen (for bag opening) 20 x 6 in (50 x 15cm)

Cotton crepe (for lining, base board fabric) 16 x 22 in (40 x 55cm)

Fusible belt interfacing $1\frac{5}{8}$ in wide x 18 in (4cm wide x 45cm)

Poly fiber (for base board) 10 x 2 in (25 x 5cm)

Punched leather tape (for handles) $\frac{5}{8}$ in wide x 36 in (1.5cm wide x 90cm)

Magnet fasteners (sew-on type) x 1 set

Hand sewing thread such as MOCO brand, pink, dark pink

Hand sewing thread such as Schappe Spun brand, red, light pink

❀ DRAFTING

※ Measurements given in inches and centimeters

※○ Add figure in circle as seam allowance when drafting pattern (①cm = $\frac{3}{8}$ in; ⑮cm = $\frac{5}{8}$ in)

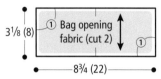

$3\frac{1}{8}$ (8)

① Bag opening fabric (cut 2) ①

$8\frac{3}{4}$ (22)

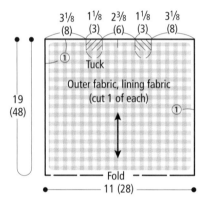

$3\frac{1}{8}$ (8) $1\frac{1}{8}$ (3) $2\frac{3}{8}$ (6) $1\frac{1}{8}$ (3) $3\frac{1}{8}$ (8)

Tuck

Outer fabric, lining fabric (cut 1 of each)

① ①

19 (48)

Fold

11 (28)

(1.5)

$1\frac{5}{8}$ (4) Base board fabric (cut 1) ←→

(1.5)

$9\frac{1}{2}$ (24)

❀ INSTRUCTIONS

1 Embroider bag opening fabric and attach adhesive belt interfacing (use dry iron on medium heat)

BAG OPENING FABRIC (RS)

Embroider (see p70 for embroidery diagram, see p55 for embroidery instructions)

$\frac{3}{8}$ (1) Attach adhesive belt interfacing

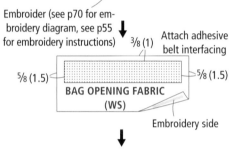

$\frac{5}{8}$ (1.5) $\frac{5}{8}$ (1.5)

BAG OPENING FABRIC (WS)

Embroidery side

Stitch magnet fasteners in place

1 (2.5)

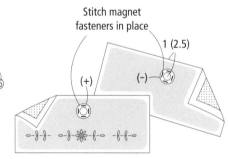

(+) (−)

2 Create tucks in outer fabric and lining fabric

$\frac{1}{4}$ (0.5)

Fold tucks and sew using running stitch

OUTER FABRIC (RS)

$\frac{1}{4}$ (0.5)

Fold tucks and sew using running stitch

LINING FABRIC (RS)

★Make markings for tucks on right side of fabric

3 Sew outer fabric and lining fabric together

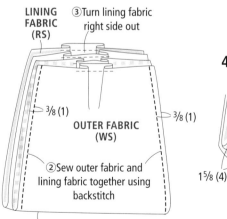

LINING FABRIC (RS) ③Turn lining fabric right side out

$\frac{3}{8}$ (1) $\frac{3}{8}$ (1)

OUTER FABRIC (WS)

②Sew outer fabric and lining fabric together using backstitch

①Fold outer fabric in half with right sides together. Do the same for lining fabric and place next to outer fabric.

4 Sew gussets on base

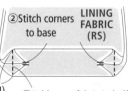

②Stitch corners to base LINING FABRIC (RS)

$1\frac{5}{8}$ (4)

①Fold outer fabric in half with right sides together. Do the same for lining fabric and place next to outer fabric.

5 Attach bag opening fabric to bag opening

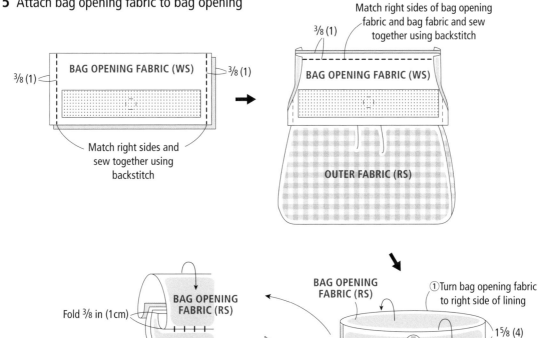

³⁄₈ (1)

³⁄₈ (1)

BAG OPENING FABRIC (WS)

³⁄₈ (1)

Match right sides and sew together using backstitch

Match right sides of bag opening fabric and bag fabric and sew together using backstitch

³⁄₈ (1)

BAG OPENING FABRIC (WS)

OUTER FABRIC (RS)

Fold ³⁄₈ in (1cm)

BAG OPENING FABRIC (RS)

OUTER FABRIC (WS)

LINING FABRIC (RS)

BAG OPENING FABRIC (RS)

① Turn bag opening fabric to right side of lining

1⁵⁄₈ (4)

② Hem stitch

LINING FABRIC (RS)

6 Turn right side out and attach straps

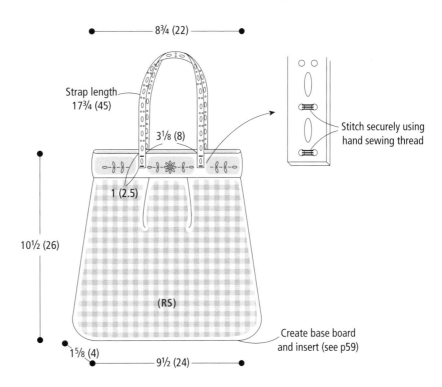

8³⁄₄ (22)

Strap length 17³⁄₄ (45)

3¹⁄₈ (8)

Stitch securely using hand sewing thread

1 (2.5)

10½ (26)

(RS)

Create base board and insert (see p59)

1⁵⁄₈ (4)

9½ (24)

79

Published in 2014 by Tuttle Publishing, an imprint of Periplus Editions (HK) Ltd.

www.tuttlepublishing.com

ISBN 978-4-8053-1316-9

Tenuide chikuchiku yawarakai bag (NV6514)
Copyright © 2008 Emiko Takahashi / NIHON VOGUE-SHA
English Translation © 2014 Periplus Editions (HK) Ltd.
Photographer: Masahito Jyugame, Kana Watanabe
Translated from Japanese by Leeyong Soo
All rights reserved.

Distributed by
North America, Latin America & Europe
Tuttle Publishing
364 Innovation Drive,
North Clarendon,
VT 05759-9436 U.S.A.
Tel: 1 (802) 773-8930
Fax: 1 (802) 773-6993
info@tuttlepublishing.com
www.tuttlepublishing.com

Japan
Tuttle Publishing
Yaekari Building,
3rd Floor, 5-4-12 Osaki,
Shinagawa-ku,
Tokyo 141 0032
Tel: (81) 3 5437-0171
Fax: (81) 3 5437-0755
sales@tuttle.co.jp
www.tuttle.co.jp

Asia Pacific
Berkeley Books Pte. Ltd.
61 Tai Seng Avenue #02-12
Singapore 534167
Tel: (65) 6280-1330
Fax: (65) 6280-6290
inquiries@periplus.com.sg
www.periplus.com

Printed in Malaysia   1408TW
17 16 15 14   6 5 4 3 2 1

The Tuttle Story
"Books to Span the East and West"

Many people are surprised to learn that the world's largest publisher of books on Asia had its humble beginnings in the tiny American state of Vermont. The company's founder, Charles E. Tuttle, belonged to a New England family steeped in publishing.

Tuttle's father was a noted antiquarian dealer in Rutland, Vermont. Young Charles honed his knowledge of the trade working in the family bookstore, and later in the rare books section of Columbia University Library. His passion for beautiful books—old and new—never wavered throughout his long career as a bookseller and publisher.

After graduating from Harvard, Tuttle enlisted in the military and in 1945 was sent to Tokyo to work on General Douglas MacArthur's staff. He was tasked with helping to revive the Japanese publishing industry, which had been utterly devastated by the war. When his tour of duty was completed, he left the military, married a talented and beautiful singer, Reiko Chiba, and in 1948 began several successful business ventures.

To his astonishment, Tuttle discovered that postwar Tokyo was actually a book-lover's paradise. He befriended dealers in the Kanda district and began supplying rare Japanese editions to American libraries. He also imported American books to sell to the thousands of GIs stationed in Japan. By 1949, Tuttle's business was thriving, and he opened Tokyo's very first English-language bookstore in the Takashimaya Department Store in Ginza, to great success. Two years later, he began publishing books to fulfill the growing interest of foreigners in all things Asian.

Though a westerner, Tuttle was hugely instrumental in bringing a knowledge of Japan and Asia to a world hungry for information about the East. By the time of his death in 1993, he had published over 6,000 books on Asian culture, history and art—a legacy honored by Emperor Hirohito in 1983 with the "Order of the Sacred Treasure," the highest honor Japan can bestow upon a non-Japanese.

The Tuttle company today maintains an active backlist of some 1,500 titles, many of which have been continuously in print since the 1950s and 1960s—a great testament to Charles Tuttle's skill as a publisher. More than 60 years after its founding, Tuttle Publishing is more active today than at any time in its history, still inspired by Charles Tuttle's core mission—to publish fine books to span the East and West and provide a greater understanding of each.